CHANGING YOUR COMPANY FROM THE INSIDE OUT

CHANGING YOUR COMPANY FROM THE INSIDE OUT

A GUIDE FOR SOCIAL INTRAPRENEURS

Gerald F. Davis and
Christopher J. White

HARVARD BUSINESS REVIEW PRESS

Boston, Massachusetts

Printed in the United States of America

10 9 8 7 6 5 4 3 2 1

The web addresses referenced in this book were live and correct at the time of the book's publication but may be subject to change.

Library of Congress Cataloging-in-Publication Data

David, Gerald F. (Gerald Fredrick), 1961-
    Changing your company from the inside out: a guide for social intrapreneurs/Gerald F. Davis and Chris White.
        pages cm
    ISBN 978-1-4221-8509-4 (hardback)
    1. Social entrepreneurship,   2. Social responsibility of business.
    3. Organizational change.   I. White, Chris, (Christopher J.)   II. Title.
    HD60.D28   2015
    658.4'08—dc23   2014037106

The paper used in this publication meets the requirements of the American National Standard for Permanence of Paper for Publications and Documents in Libraries and Archives Z39.48-1992.

ISBN: 9781422185094
eISBN: 9781422185100

To the memory of Mayer N. Zald,
our friend and mentor

Contents

Preface

Changing Your Company from the Inside Out started with a challenge. Back then, Chris was a new MBA student, Jerry was a grizzled faculty veteran, and we wanted to design a course that would teach students how to make positive change in the world through business. Social entrepreneurship had become trendy, and there were plenty of books and cases on the topic. Yet few MBA students were in a financial position to head directly from their degree program to a nonprofit or to create their own start-up social enterprise; most would end up in mainstream corporate jobs, no matter how passionate they were about social change. The challenge was to teach business students how to be effective change agents from within the corporate world.

We set out to meet with people who had been particularly effective at leading social impact initiatives within their companies. Across dozens of conversations, we asked them what they wished they had learned in business school to be effective at advancing a social impact agenda at work. Their answers persuaded us that the tools used in social movements applied to the corporate world as well. Reading the organization's climate to know when the time was right for an innovation, using language and stories that positively disposed people toward the idea, recruiting the right allies and avoiding blockers, and using forums that allowed the group to work together effectively were common to both. Lessons from social movement activism could be adapted to the corporate setting. The result was our MBA course on social intrapreneurship, which quickly attracted an enthusiastic audience, executive programs on selling issues internally, and this book.

We draw on excellent research and theory about issue selling, intrapreneurship, and social movements from many colleagues and friends, including Jane Dutton, Sue Ashford, and the late Mayer Zald. Yet our goal is entirely practical. This book is about tools you can use now and throughout your career to lead change from any seat in an organization. It is both concrete and topical. We consider "Use this specific software to analyze the social network structure of your department to locate connectors and mavens" to be much more useful advice than "Follow your passion." And we note both the prospects and pitfalls of using information and communication technologies within a corporate setting to bring about change.

CHANGING YOUR YOUR COMPANY FROM THE INSIDE OUT

CHAPTER ONE

How Can I Pay the Bills and Still Live My Values?

A corporate job does not have to be a compromise between earning your paycheck and sticking to your values.

In fact, changing what big businesses do can have a much larger impact than founding a social enterprise. Digging a well in a low-income village can have a positive effect in that village. But persuading a multinational manufacturer to adopt a formal commitment to fresh water access as a basic human right, as David Berdish did at Ford, can be transformative. Getting a large consumer packaged goods company to source raw materials from farmers in Rwanda, as Justin DeKoszmovszky did, can foster sustainable economic development. Creating an online marketplace for artisans in low-income communities to sell their goods to rich-world consumers via eBay, as Robert Chatwani did, can create new opportunities globally.

Berdish, DeKoszmovszky, and Chatwani found themselves at different points in their careers as their social innovations took hold. Berdish was well into his career at Ford, for example, while DeKoszmovszky was an MBA intern when he first started influencing change within his company. The three operated in different industries—automotive, consumer goods, and internet technology, respectively. Their initiatives have been wide-ranging, impacting human rights policies around the world, starting new businesses alongside some of the poorest people in the world, and creating access to new, affluent customers for disconnected artisans. This is what social intrapreneurs do: they work within existing organizations to make positive social change.

But there may be a tension between our day jobs and our values. Feminists working in male-dominated Wall Street firms, environmentalists working at energy companies, vegetarians working for packaged food companies—all find conflicts between their own values and where they work. Yet it is these tensions that present the opportunity for social intrapreneurs to make radical change in the world. Debra Meyerson at Stanford and Maureen Scully at the University of Massachusetts coined the phrase *tempered radicals* to describe individuals who were strongly committed to social values, yet were able to operate effectively in a corporate setting.[1] Meyerson and Scully described the tensions this created and how many of these individuals were able to be true to themselves and create change without getting fired. They had found answers to the question "How can I pay my bills and still live my values?"

Changing Your Company from the Inside Out provides a practical toolkit for creating positive social change within a corporate setting. We walk through the when, why, who, and how of social innovation, drawing on the experiences of social innovators in varied settings, from multinational corporations to the Arab Spring. We describe a systematic set of steps that you can take to recognize an opportunity for introducing a social innovation; to use the right language and stories to pitch the innovation to different audiences; to map the network of social relationships at work in order to locate potential allies to recruit to your effort—and opponents to avoid; and to use the right platform to collaborate effectively.

We also introduce useful online tools that allow innovations to go big. Recent social movements have demonstrated how social media can accelerate the speed and expand the reach of contagious messages and allow dispersed individuals around the world to work together for change. But other online tools can also aid innovators. Content analysis software can scan corporate texts such as annual reports, letters to shareholders, and recruiting materials to yield insights into the company's culture, suggesting what kinds of arguments and stories are likely to be persuasive. Network analysis software can use available information from staffing records, LinkedIn or Twitter accounts, or e-mail traces to map and quantify the social network at work. This can aid in recruiting allies and uncover the shortest paths to decision makers.

Where Do Social Innovations Come From?

There is no guidebook for how Ford Motor Company should respond to the HIV epidemic in South Africa, where it has significant manufacturing operations, or how Goldman Sachs should take on issues of gender inequality, which have particular resonance on Wall Street.

Companies blindsided by change often had the materials for a response within their own boundaries. The Xerox Palo Alto Research Center (PARC), a major innovator in computer science, famously invented many of the features that wound up in the Apple Macintosh—but not in any Xerox products—including the mouse and the graphical user interface. Eastman Kodak was an early innovator in digital imaging, including digital cameras, decades before its bankruptcy in 2013. Nokia had plans for touchscreen smartphones and tablet computers years before Apple introduced the iPhone and iPad. Yet for a number of reasons articulated by Clay Christensen—pressures from current customers and suppliers, not wanting to cannibalize existing businesses, or simple uncertainty—these companies often fail to pursue innovations vigorously.[2]

The same thing is true for making the most of social change. Companies may fail to pursue it. A company's own employees are often the best source—and advocates—for adaptive innovations.

We know from experience that managers at the grassroots level are often acutely aware of, say, opportunities for greener production methods, triple-bottom-line services that the firm could be selling using its existing resources, community benefits that the company could be providing at low cost, or human rights issues in the supply chain. Poet Ezra Pound wrote that "Artists are the antennae of the race," the "registering instruments" for what is to come.[3] In the same way, employees are connected to the social waves that the corporation will be encountering, and can anticipate and respond before those at the top know what's about to hit them. The people in the

C-suite may not have an unvarnished view of how their company is viewed by the public, or whether sourcing cocoa from Ivory Coast will tarnish their reputation, but their recently hired MBAs coming back from a recruiting visit know.

The solutions to such issues often reside within the organization itself. Many companies are overflowing with grassroots social innovations, ideas for products or practices that serve business purposes while making a social contribution. Yet these initiatives are often smothered in the crib. Even successful intrapreneurs often find themselves swimming against the tide of organizational culture. Accenture's Gib Bulloch refers to the "corporate antibodies" that "kill off anything that doesn't look 'normal.'" IBM's Kevin Thompson described how the idea for a "corporate Peace Corps" was initially considered laughable. Big Blue is a business, not a foreign aid office. It can't cure all of the world's ills and also keep its shareholders happy.[4]

Yet failing to innovate socially is no longer an option for any major corporation.

Corporations face a balancing act—encouraging social innovations that allow them to be adaptable while not becoming distracted by every possibility. Some level of corporate antibodies is essential. Some proposed innovations are simply bad ideas; others are lower priority. What is critical, however, is that companies create a climate in which ideas get a hearing. This is not a commitment to climbing every new mountain, but to being open to the possibility of innovation. Whole Foods Market, for instance, concluded that plastic grocery bags—which are used only once but live on in landfills or oceans for centuries—were simply not sustainable, and that consumers could be persuaded to switch to paper or bring their own reusable bags. Thus, in early 2008, plastic bags disappeared forever from Whole

Foods stores. This is the kind of initiative that the company wants to promote: it is non-obvious, and indeed angered some customers, but it is consistent with the culture and has proven to be infectious within the industry. More and more people are showing up at stores with reusable bags and keeping a stock of them in the trunks of their cars—it has become normal. We learned from co-CEO Walter Robb that the company has dozens of other potentially great ideas on the docket for consideration at any given time. Of course, they can't all be winners, but this is the worthwhile price Whole Foods pays to being open to social innovation.

Innovation and Social Movements

Leading social innovations in organizations is a lot like leading a social movement. Social movements are organized efforts to make change in some aspect of society. They come in sizes large (the Arab Spring), medium (*Kony 2012*), and small (a virtual movement on Facebook to reinstate a fired cashier at Applebee's). They emerge from the political right (the Tea Party), left (Occupy Wall Street), and center (No Labels), and some are not especially political at all. And they are pervasive: all of these movements came about within the past five years, and new ones seem to materialize almost daily, although not all of them are effective.

Social innovations in society often result from the actions of social movements; for example, the creation of consumer watchdogs like Consumers Union, the spread of alternative dispute resolution, and health maintenance organizations (HMOs). The social landscape is plentifully populated with other examples.[5]

The same is true for social innovations in organizations. Research by Maureen Scully, Doug Creed, Huggy Rao, and others has found that changes in corporate practice are often the result of social movements among employees.[6] Consider *domestic partner benefits*—health insurance and other benefits offered to partners of LGBT employees, equivalent to those offered to straight married employees. In 1990, these benefits were almost entirely absent from the corporate world. The notion that all employees should have access to the same benefits, regardless of the configuration of their family, was unheard-of, if not unthinkable. When Jerry was living in New York in the mid-1990s, he connected with another dad at a playground when their kids were playing together and fell into conversation about domestic partner benefits, which Jerry's colleagues Doug and Maureen were researching. As it happened, the other dad worked at a well-known financial company where he himself was leading an effort to implement domestic partner benefits. His job put him in regular contact with the CEO, who held attitudes from a previous generation. The task was clear, if not easy: gather enough supporters among employees, some of whom may have been reluctant to make clear that this issue was important to them and would yield benefits for recruiting and retention (the business case); allay concerns that this would be too costly or would alienate customers; and provide examples of other companies that had adopted domestic partner benefits to show precedent. It would help to have vivid personal examples of how adopting this benefit improved peoples' lives, and perhaps cautionary tales of what failing to adopt would mean for employees. This was not just a business decision: this was about the company's core values around equity and inclusion.

And it was not just a change effort, like adopting Six Sigma: it was a social movement.

Successful social movements tend to follow a playbook that can be seen as answers to four questions:

- *When* is the right time for change?

- *Why* is this a compelling change?

- *Who* should be involved?

- *How* should they organize to press for change?

Although the questions are straightforward, their answers often require considerable finesse. Movements do not always arise where one expects, which prompts political commentators to lament, "Where is the outrage?"

Our master hypothesis in this book is that movements for innovation are more successful to the extent that all of these factors—when, why, who, and how—are aligned. That is, intrapreneurs will be more successful when their innovation is proposed at the right time, using the right rationale for the right people, who are connected by the right platform. What counts as "right," of course, is highly variable. But figuring that out is the point of this book.

There are several recurring motifs in the book. We will move back and forth between society and organizations, in the belief that there is a strong analogy between them. We will also be returning to the theme that information technology changes everything.

One of the reasons that movements seem so common today is that information and communication technologies have dissolved many of the barriers to organizing. The 1963 March on Washington that featured Martin Luther King Jr.'s famous "I Have a Dream" speech took months to organize and no small amount of postage, printing, phone calls, car pools, and physical coordination. The 2011 protest in Cairo's Tahrir Square that ousted Hosni Mubarak took mere days to organize, thanks largely to mobile phones and the internet.

Social innovators in the corporate world can learn from social movement activists, a point we attribute to our late friend and mentor Mayer Zald.[7] Methods that work to change governments can, on a smaller scale, change organizations. Both often face opposition and inertia; both are now made easier by technology.

This idea is, at first blush, preposterous. Are we arguing that someone who leads an effort to reduce carbon emissions in the supply chain can claim the mantle of Rosa Parks? Is a company's community engagement initiative really all that similar to Occupy Wall Street, or the Tea Party movement? Our answer is *no*, you are not Rosa Parks, but *yes*, social innovators can be kindred to early members of Occupy or the Tea Party. Social intrapreneurs are heroic in their own way, but they rarely put their personal safety on the line—although there are career risks to intrapreneurship. On the other hand, successful social innovations generally require coordinated group action, and in this sense, leading a social initiative follows the same rules as launching a social movement. Just as CEOs can learn from the experiences of generals and political leaders, social intrapreneurs can learn from the experience of contemporary social movements.

Business in a Time of Social Change

It's not just individuals who should care about these opportunities. Business must care too. According to some observers, businesses now need to earn their "license to operate" by demonstrating their social value.

Sometimes this is encoded into regulation and statute. Banks seeking approval for mergers in the United States often must document that they have reinvested in their communities, which is one of the reason's that expansion-minded banks are among the most generous philanthropists in the business world. In other cases, the requirement to be socially responsible is more implicit. Some companies take on this responsibility with gusto, creating departments of social responsibility and publicly touting their good works.

But there is a flip side as well. Corporations find that they cannot be innocent bystanders or claim ignorance. They are drawn into conflicts over social issues that they might have preferred to avoid. Thanks to the Dodd-Frank Act of 2010, corporations listed on American stock markets are now required to disclose if their products contain "conflict minerals" that may have originated from the Democratic Republic of the Congo (DRC), as many electronics do. They are not required to avoid such minerals, but to document if, through the purchases of supplies or components containing minerals from the DRC, they are inadvertently funding armed conflict. Of course, such minerals are typically many steps back in the supply chain, and few companies had any idea whether their products contained, say, tantalum or tungsten from DRC. Yet some have been accused of producing "genocide phones."

Consider the plight of Howard Schultz, CEO of Starbucks. Starbucks had a policy of following local laws on carrying firearms in the open, and in 2013 it became the unbidden beneficiary of "Starbucks Appreciation Day." Gun owners had organized online to visit their local Starbucks with their firearms on prominent display, including at the store in Newtown, Connecticut—site of a horrific school shooting the previous year.[8] Schultz responded with an open letter "respectfully requesting that customers no longer bring firearms into our stores or outdoor seating areas—even in states where 'open carry' is permitted—unless they are authorized law enforcement personnel." It was not a ban, because Schultz did not want to "require our partners to confront armed customers," but a respectful request.[9]

Schultz was clear: Starbucks was not a policy maker, not pro- or anti-gun. It was the job of the legislature to make gun laws, not the job of Starbucks. Yet the company could not easily escape this bind, which was forced upon it by circumstance. And Starbucks had previously taken a highly visible stand in favor of marriage equality in its home state of Washington, suggesting that their aversion to taking policy stances was not universal.[10]

In contrast, Brendan Eich had been CEO of Mozilla for only two weeks when he resigned under pressure in April 2014. Although Eich was a well-regarded technologist and cofounder of Mozilla, his financial support of California's Proposition 8 in 2008, banning same-sex marriage, prompted controversy inside and outside the company. Employee sentiment against the appointment was evidenced by a storm of tweets expressing unhappiness with Eich's position. At least one employee went on unpaid leave in protest. Outside the company, those who visited dating site OKCupid using Mozilla's Firefox browser were informed of Eich's opposition to marriage equality and encouraged to return via a different browser. Eich was evidently unwilling to recant his support for Proposition 8, leaving his departure as the only feasible course of action.[11]

Conflicts like this are certain to become increasingly common as companies are expected to take stands on issues and to incorporate practices into their operations that address societal questions—particularly those that arouse their employees' interest. Corporations today face a "responsibility paradox": their operations are often dispersed around the globe and their supply chains extend far beyond their line of sight, yet they are now held accountable for more activities beyond their boundaries. At a time when corporations increasingly rely on far-flung vendors to assemble and distribute their goods, they are also seen as responsible for the actions of their broader enterprise. Nike and Apple are expected to vouch for the labor practices of their suppliers, and to be answerable when those practices do not measure up. Disney and H&M are regarded as complicit when unauthorized subcontractors for their vendors in Bangladesh manufacture under dangerous conditions. Oil companies such as Unocal have been held liable for the actions of the governments of the countries where they do business.[12]

Moreover, on a day-to-day basis, corporate employers that hope to attract and retain the most skilled and creative workers are expected to provide a just and rewarding climate. A paycheck alone is not enough. "No justice, no peace" has morphed into "No justice, no PowerPoint presentation," or "No justice, no Python code."

Professional service firms in accounting and consulting have long been in the vanguard of offering benefits and workplace practices that support diversity. Take domestic partner benefits. In the days before the move to marriage equality, LGBT employees' partners were unable to access employee benefits. In the early 1990s, a handful of high-tech and professional service companies began offering domestic partner benefits to address this inequity, in part to compete for valued talent. By 2013, even Walmart began providing domestic partner benefits, finding that it was nearly the last one in its industry to do so. What had been a bold and controversial statement favoring diversity twenty years before was now almost obligatory for America's largest, and perhaps most conventional, employer.[13]

What Will You Get out of This Book?

Changing Your Company from the Inside Out is a guide for social intrapreneurs who want to make a positive difference through their organizations. Join us as we draw the parallels between the courageous activists on the streets of Cairo and the audacious change agents striving to make a positive change from their cubicles within some of the world's best-known companies. While contexts are different, we expect you will find that you have more in common than you might have realized. Indeed, you might conclude that you can learn much from each other. We provide the four essential steps for leading change at any station in society, and any seat in an organization.

CHAPTER TWO

Four Kinds of Social Innovation in Organizations

Intrapreneurs often don't label themselves as such. The term *intrapreneur* was, as far as we can tell, first proposed by two academics, neither of whom were social change agents.[1] We can only imagine that the social change agents themselves might have come up with a more artful term. In fact, as we will see in later chapters, the best intrapreneurs create descriptions of their initiatives that attract allies without seeming overtly threatening to those who might actively oppose them. However, as far as we are concerned, it remains the naming equivalent of democracy in the eyes of Sir Winston Churchill: the worst imaginable, apart from all the others.

Our working definition is this:

> *Social intrapreneurs lead change within their organizations, without formal authority, that aligns with core business*

objectives while also advancing a social or environmental outcome.

What Do Social Innovations in Organizations Look Like?

Social intrapreneurship has three consistent features:

Source: Social innovations are initiated by someone who is not the final decision maker. The idea originates from outside his or her direct area of accountability. Otherwise, this is not intrapreneurship; it is just doing your job.

Purpose: Social innovations create positive social or environmental outcomes *while advancing core business objectives.* Notice that we are saying "core business objectives," not profit. This is a broader lens than is often used. Retention of great employees, for example, is something that advances core business objectives. If the initiative does not advance social or environmental objectives, it is not *social* intrapreneurship; it is just intrapreneurship.

Nature: Social innovations are capable of being institutionalized into the way the company works; they are not just one-off initiatives. As we'll see, intrapreneurs often start with pilot programs and initiatives to gain early traction for their ideas. However, they quickly escalate to gain widespread support for their efforts. They embed the initiatives into the processes and structures of the company such that they are able to survive and continue despite the inevitable changes in the organizational power structures.

Categories of Social Innovation

From our discussions with intrapreneurs and background research, we find there are four broad kinds of social innovation in organizations. As is traditional in business schools, we gave them alliterative titles: products (and services), people, practices, and public. Some initiatives fall into more than one category, but we find this to be a helpful schema for thinking about the wide range of possibilities for impact while advancing core business objectives.

Products

Social innovations in products and services improve the lot of the environment, the community, or the employees of the company and are offered to the outside world in return for payment. You could think about these as social enterprises sprouting up within a larger organization.

eBay World of Good

Like many Indian expatriates, Robert Chatwani loves to reconnect with the color, vibrancy, and energy of the bazaars when he visits his family home. On a 2004 visit, Chatwani—then a young internet marketing manager at eBay—stopped by a bustling market in Ahmedabad with his family. Intrigued by the beautiful wares and surprisingly low prices, Chatwani started to conceive of a business idea. He bought some gold jewelry for $700 and took it back to his San Jose home to undertake an experiment—he sold that jewelry for $1,200 on eBay within a few weeks.

eBay itself has social innovation in its DNA. Pierre Omidyar famously founded the company to help his wife buy and sell PEZ candy dispensers. Soon, though, eBay evolved to reflect Omidyar's vision for a world where economic opportunity was enabled by more open and accessible markets. These values, and eBay's deep capabilities of building online marketplaces, provided an unusually good match for someone as entrepreneurial and idealistic as Robert Chatwani.

Thrilled by the result of his experiment, Chatwani saw a broader opportunity. Over the next three years, he worked alongside his day job to create a new business model with wide-ranging positive impacts for customers, artisans, and communities. The result was the World of Good fair trade marketplace.

World of Good was an online platform where consumers could buy products from artisans from around the world. The goods were certified by "Trust Providers"—fair trade associations and certification groups—with various categories of impact: Planet Positive meant it was good for the environment; People Positive for people, and so forth. The artisans gained access to new markets and a higher price point. The consumers got access to beautifully handcrafted products—and the knowledge that their dollars were making a positive impact in the world.

Over time, World of Good came to be housed within a social innovation hotbed: the Global Citizenship function at eBay. MicroPlace, for instance, is a marketplace that facilitates microlending to entrepreneurs. eBay Giving Works supports distributed and decentralized workplace philanthropy programs. These social initiatives are distinct from eBay's philanthropic programs. Social innovations are intended to be financially sustainable and to funnel revenue back into Global Citizenship to create more social innovation platforms such as these. In 2013, the artisanal fair-trade products that had been offered on the stand-alone World of Good portal were integrated into the main eBay marketplace. In chapter 5, we will share some of the specific tactics that Robert Chatwani employed to sell his social innovation at eBay.

Other "product" social innovations include:

- Bloomberg integrated environmental, social, and governance (ESG) metrics into its ubiquitous terminals. By doing so, it gives investors the chance to make investments based on a broader range of metrics than expected financial return.

- We were thrilled when Whole Foods Market entered Detroit, and in so doing opened the only national grocery chain within the city limits. The size of the store, the supplier network, and the price point are among the variables that Whole Foods customized to extend access to healthy foods in a financially sustainable manner that would benefit consumers, employees, and local food suppliers in Detroit.

- Lower-fuel-emission cars reduce environmental impact, save consumers money, and generate profit for the manufacturer. Toyota and Ford are among those leading the way at the moment, and we expect that this market will continue to grow.

People

Social innovations for people aim to create a more just and rewarding workplace for employees. Sub-optimal workplace conditions are sadly all too common. Many of us who have spent sufficient time in organizations will have had moments where we are thriving, but it is also more than likely we have also witnessed or experienced incivility, discrimination, inequality, or simply poor management. Some groups face systemic challenges to getting and growing a rewarding and meaningful career because of economic, gender, or racial differences.

Welfare-to-Career at Cascade Engineering

Michigan-based Cascade Engineering is a hotbed of social innovation. From its founding forty years ago, and long before it was considered sexy to do so, Cascade has worked toward a triple bottom line, and it was one of the first manufacturers to become a certified B Corporation—one that meets set social sustainability and environmental performance, accountability, and transparency standards. Founder and former CEO Fred Keller carries around in his wallet a well-thumbed quotation attributed to eighteenth-century theologian John Wesley:

> *Do all the good you can*
> *By all the means you can,*
> *In all the ways you can,*
> *In all the places you can,*
> *At all the times you can,*
> *To all the people you can,*
> *As long as ever you can.*

The environment at Cascade is clearly friendly to social innovation, and Keller leads by example. Sometimes, challenging business environments create the catalyst for social innovation. In the early 1990s, Cascade noted that local unemployment was sometimes exceptionally low in the area around Cascade's main production facilities and that turnover increased dramatically when it tried to hire from traditional employment pools. One day while walking through the factory, Keller stopped to talk to Ron Jimmerson, a machine operator, who told the CEO that he had an interest in helping people get hired from non-traditional sources. This started a series of actions over the next decade that would ultimately lead to Jimmerson playing key roles as a human resources manager and community relations leader and establishing a program that would help those on long-term welfare to find a job, and then a career at Cascade.

The first edition of the Welfare-to-Career program, in 1991, was very simple. Cascade put on a van service for eight home-less men who wanted to come from the homeless shelter to work at the company. It didn't work. It turned out that trans-portation wasn't the reason why people weren't working. One of the challenges that version 1.0 of the program had revealed was the difficulty of helping people get accustomed to the new routines and discipline that came with beginning their first professional job, or returning after a long time out.

A few years passed and then Cascade partnered with Stuart Ray, a friend of Keller's and the owner of several local Burger Kings. The participants were given a job at one of Ray's restau-rants, and they were promised a chance to progress to a man-ufacturing job at Cascade if they qualified. Version 2.0 did not work either. This time, the Cascade team learned that the participants working at Burger King had so many barriers to overcome that giving them an opportunity to work was not enough—they needed additional support. So Cascade part-nered with government and non-profit organizations to provide services "in-house," trained its supervisors to understand the unspoken "hidden rules" of class differences, and even put supervisors through poverty-simulation training.[2]

By 1998, a third version of the Welfare-to-Career program started to emerge. This time, the Cascade team treated the program not just as a hiring and retention tactic, but as a system that improved the culture throughout the company. With this broader goal in mind, it was easier for the company to justify the investments needed to engage a wider support system of partners for the participants. This eventually included paying for the time of a Michigan Department of Human Services caseworker, Joyce Gutierrez-Marsh, who maintained an office on-site. Having a caseworker available to all employees made it easier to address some of the distinctive needs of those transitioning from public assistance, which were often beyond the reach of Cascade management.

In time—and thanks to the skill and persistence of the Cascade team and the participants—the investments paid off. At a human level, hundreds of people have been able to make the transition from welfare to a career—with the dignity, confidence, and increased economic prospects that entails. The program made good business sense for Cascade. Average monthly turnover within the Welfare-to-Career program fell from 62 percent in 2000 to 3 percent by 2009. Cascade saved millions of dollars by reducing turnover costs during this nine-year period. The state of Michigan also saved a fortune from people coming off welfare support. Most importantly, according to Keller, was the fact that investing in people on chronic welfare showed that Cascade cared about all of its employees very deeply, enhancing its reputation as an employer for those at all employment levels.

Sometimes, innovations take time to stick. We might be lulled by our success stories into believing that new initiatives either work or don't work in a relatively short time frame. In reality, the glow of many of the best social innovations disguises the fact that their success came about after years of trial and error—and many false starts. Keller is quick to note that the path to success for the Welfare-to-Career program was not linear and that many of its benefits were not those at planned its outset. The programs pioneered by Ron Jimmerson epitomize the value of perseverance and persistence in creating new social innovations—in this case, applied to creating a more supportive work environment while meeting business objectives. Often, intrapreneurs have multiple initiatives underway at the same time. At certain times, one initiative in their portfolio will be gaining traction. At other times, it will be in an incubation period while other initiatives accelerate.

Other social innovations for people include:

- Extending the same benefits to same-sex domestic partners as are offered to partners within a traditional marriage relationship.

- Creation of leadership development programs with social impact, such as volunteer programs or time allotted for volunteer efforts, increase connection with the community, while increasing employee engagement and happiness.

Practices

Social innovations in processes alter the way the company operates to be better for the environment, the community, or the people working within the company—while advancing a core business objective.

Ford's Code of Human Rights

At its May 2003 Centennial Shareholders Meeting, Ford Motor Company announced the development of Ford's Code of Basic Working Conditions as part of its commitment to corporate citizenship and making the world a better place. The Code was written and developed by a cross-functional team with assistance from external stakeholders. It is based on the fundamental elements of internationally recognized labor standards, including the UN Declaration of Human Rights, the International Labor Organization Covenants, and the UN Global Compact.

David Berdish, a sustainability manager at Ford, led the development of the Code. Berdish is a disarming guy. He radiates warmth and kindness straight away to those who meet him. Yet you don't have to wait long to realize that Berdish is a straight shooter, able to deliver hard messages in appropriate ways to corporate top brass just as clearly and effectively as he is able to relate to the guys just getting off their production shift. Berdish's results as a corporate change agent will stand the test of time. The Code was integrated into all decision making at Ford, and provides an ethical decision-making framework that accounts for the communities in which it works and the way its employees are treated. Even with a supply chain as far-reaching as Ford's, proactive implementation of this code has enabled the company to avoid many of the pitfalls experienced by other manufacturing companies with extensive emerging market operations. It has helped the car manufacturer become one of the most admired companies for social sustainability.

Ford is the first company in the automotive industry to develop its own code of ethical conduct, and the only company to train, assess, audit, and remediate within its first-tier supply base. In 2007, Ford became part of the UN Global Compact, and is the only manufacturer to be part of the UN Human Rights Working Group. In 2012, Ford revised its policy to include a commitment to the elimination of conflict minerals, trafficking, and environmental justice, including access to water as a fundamental human right.

Assessment of Ford facilities and its partners began in 2004. The purchasing organization is also working with Ford suppliers to comply with human rights codes of its own, including specific terms and conditions, supplier training courses, and third-party audits, especially in China, Mexico, Turkey, Russia, Romania, and India.

We will learn from David Berdish's experiences in developing and implementing Ford's Code of Human Rights in chapters 4 and 8.

Other examples of social innovation in organizational practices include:

- Greening the supply chain—reducing waste and environmental footprint—saves companies many millions of dollars a year, while reducing environmental impact and creating a halo effect with customers.

- Green teams—self-organizing bands of employees working to reduce the environmental impact of company operations—save money, reduce environmental impact, and increase employee engagement.

Public

Social innovation at the boundaries where the business meets the interests of the public allow companies to support the interests of other stakeholders, while advancing core business objectives.

IBM's Corporate Service Corps

It is not easy to stay true to your values and identity when working in a big, publicly traded company. Kevin Thompson would know.[3] When Thompson first proposed the idea of a program inspired by the Peace Corps at IBM, he was almost laughed out of the conference room. Thompson was not your cookie-cutter IBMer. Big Blue, culturally, can be quite buttoned down, very driven by the bottom line. With his mop of blond hair, Thompson looks younger and less experienced than he is. When he entered IBM, he had an MBA from Cornell, but his main experiences had been as a volunteer with the Peace Corps and traveling the world to play saxophone in a ska band. So his idea stuck out like a sore thumb. Yet due to subsequent changes in the operating context of the company and Thompson's skill and persistence, the idea gained traction.

IBM's Corporate Service Corps takes high-performing managers and places them in teams on projects with nonprofits in strategic emerging markets. The team members apply their skills and expertise to help the organization, at the same time gaining exposure to a new market and increasing their attachment to IBM as an organization. For example, a hundred or so people would be selected from an applicant pool of up-and-coming leaders from different functions and geographies within IBM. The team would be deployed to a strategic, but often early-stage, emerging market for a four-week assignment. Typical projects are consulting to local governments, schools, and nonprofits—organizations that would never otherwise be able to afford the services of one of the most prestigious firms in the world. Participants come from over fifty countries and have served communities in Argentina, Brazil, Cambodia, Chile, China, Colombia, Egypt, Ethiopia, Ghana, India, Indonesia, Kazakhstan, Kenya, Malaysia, Mexico, Morocco, Nigeria, Peru, the Philippines, Poland, Romania, Russia, Senegal, South Africa, Sri Lanka, Taiwan, Tanzania, Thailand, Tunisia, Turkey, Vietnam, UAE, and Ukraine.

In fewer than five years, the Corporate Service Corps grew to impact over 2,400 participants and an estimated 140,000 people in communities around the world. It has been named one of the Top 100 innovations in IBM's hundred-year history, and has become a best practice in talent retention and development that other large corporations continue to emulate. Thompson himself transitioned out of the Corporate Service Corps success story and continues to move up the corporate ladder at Big Blue.

What tactics did Thompson employ to move a "corporate Peace Corps" from being a fringe idea to one of IBM's most talked-about programs? We will look at this in subsequent chapters.

Other social innovations to strengthen the relationship with the public while advancing business interests include:

- Some companies, such as Ford, have taken an especially thoughtful approach to operating in at-risk communities.

For instance, David Berdish, whom we met earlier in this chapter, integrated "access to water" as a basic human right in its Code of Human Rights. This is especially important since Ford is undertaking water-intensive manufacturing operations in countries like India, where there is severe water scarcity and limited regulation of business.

- For two years before Whole Foods entered Detroit, a much lower-income economic area than its typical market, it convened community meetings to listen to the needs and concerns of their potential customers and suppliers. It organized classes for people to learn how to eat healthily on a tight budget and provided training for suppliers seeking to become qualified to sell to Whole Foods.

Conclusion

Over the past several years, we have been privileged to hear these stories, and many more, of social intrapreneurs creating change in their organizations. The changes they bring about advance core business strategies while having meaningfully positive social and environmental impacts. In the coming chapters, we will explore how these come to be in practice— why some succeed and others fail.

CHAPTER THREE

Overview of the Social Movement Framework

The March on Washington for Jobs and Justice on August 28, 1963, was a high-water mark of the American civil rights movement. Hundreds of thousands of citizens gathered around the reflecting pool in front of the Lincoln Memorial in 1963 to hear Dr. Martin Luther King Jr. share his dream. Within two years, the central pillars of the American apartheid system that had stood for nearly a century crumbled. The federal government stepped in to strike down legalized racial discrimination, from mundane exclusionary practices at hotels and restaurants to wholesale disenfranchisement of African American voters. The victories of the civil rights movement signaled that even long-standing inequities might be open to change.

The Arab Spring, which began in late 2010, saw unelected leaders toppled in state after state, from Tunisia to Egypt to

Libya. The results were not always unequivocal victories for democracy, but their scale and effect suggested that something new was afoot.

In the United States, the Tea Party movement emerged in early 2009 in response to concerns about federal spending and perceived government overreach, and within eighteen months, nearly 30 percent of voters identified themselves as Tea Party supporters. In fall 2011, the Occupy Wall Street movement arose in New York City to draw attention to rampant social inequality and the disproportionate power of finance, and rapidly spread to encampments in hundreds of cities around the world.

It is not just large-scale social issues that draw the attention of social movements. When, on a Tuesday evening in early 2012, the Susan G. Komen for the Cure foundation announced that it would no longer fund breast-cancer screenings for low-income women at Planned Parenthood, an online movement arose almost instantly on Facebook and Twitter. Hundreds of thousands of virtual protestors joined Facebook pages that decried the move or sent tweets to their followers seeking support for a boycott. Faced with a potentially catastrophic loss of external support and widespread discontent at its regional offices, the Foundation changed course on Friday, reinstating the funding and noting the departure of several senior officers.[1] Even modest changes in corporate policies, such as mobile phone pricing plans, can rouse large-scale opposition in virtual forums like Facebook, as many businesses have discovered to their dismay.

Groups like these, which are motivated by a common desire for change, can be mobilized to achieve remarkable things, often catalyzed by the actions of social movement entrepreneurs. The methods these entrepreneurs use have lessons for social intrapreneurs as well, as we learned from connecting with successful innovators. Effective social movements generally follow a common playbook. In this chapter, we provide an overview of that playbook and how it applies within organizations.

Where do these movements come from, and why are there so many of them now? First, a definition: according to Wikipedia (itself arguably a product of a social movement), social movements are "large, sometimes informal, groupings of individuals or organizations which focus on specific political or social issues . . . they carry out, resist or undo a social change."[2] Not everything done by informal groups counts as a social movement. Fashion does not count as a social movement. Pickup basketball games are not social movements. Movements require efforts at social change, which may be large (the civil rights movement or the Arab Spring) or small (an effort to reinstate a hostess at a "fast casual" restaurant chain who was fired for sharing a snarky customer's comments on social media).

Social scientists have made great progress in understanding the origins of movements and what makes them more or less successful. Some of what they have found is surprising. We might expect to see movements rise and fall in response to the level of grievance in society. Occasionally, protests arise in direct response to a particular event, such as a court decision or an instance of brutality. But the civil rights movement reached its ascendance after almost a century of Jim Crow and legal discrimination.

We might expect activists to be those with the strongest commitment to a cause. But often those who are most involved are those who share social ties to other activists, not those who feel most strongly. So scholars of social movements have created a framework to understand when, why, and how movements arise, and who gets involved. We present a distilled framework that draws on the work of Charles Tilly, Mayer Zald, John McCarthy, Doug McAdam, and others.[3] There are many theories of social movements, and our approach is aimed not at spurring research but at providing a guide to action. We adapt this framework here to the agenda and concrete problems faced by social intrapreneurs.

The Social Movement Framework for Organizational Innovation

In brief, the social movement framework is organized around four questions:

- **When?** What makes the time right for a movement? This aspect is conventionally referred to as the *opportunity structure* and focuses on what it is about events inside or outside the organization that make it more or less inviting to champion an innovation. "When" is about *opportunities*.

- **Why?** What is the compelling case for an innovation or change that will persuade potential supporters and overcome resisters? This aspect is called *framing* and refers to the overall framework, language, and stories that connect the innovation to an organization's mission, strategy, and values (or, in some circles, its *narrative*). "Why" is about *framing*.

- **Who?** Who are the innovation's potential allies and supporters, and how can you enroll them in your movement?

Who are the decision makers you need to persuade? Who are the potential roadblocks you need to steer around or neutralize? "Who" is about *networks*.

- **How?** What kind of online or offline tools and platforms can help supporters collaborate to support the innovation? "How" is about *mobilizing*.

These four questions help focus attention on the different parts that come together (or not) to make a movement successful (or not). Changes in opportunity structures, frames, networks, and mobilizing structures alter a movement's potential to launch.

A theme of this book is that one of the reasons social movements seem so much more prevalent and "infectious" today is that changes in technology—particularly advances in information and communication technologies (ICTs) such as the internet, low-cost computing, and mobile telephony—have made it easier for mobilizing groups to act toward a common interest and expand the range of formats that this mobilization can take.

This idea was the major claim of Clay Shirky's book *Here Comes Everybody*, and has been echoed or contested by others. As Shirky put it, "The centrality of group effort to human life means that anything that changes the way groups function will have profound ramifications for everything from commerce and government to media and religion. . . . Most of the barriers to group action have collapsed, and without these barriers, we are free to explore new ways of gathering together and getting things done."[4]

We do not argue that the World Wide Web is ushering in a cyber-utopia of globalized grassroots democracy. But it is indisputable that the Web, smartphones, social media, and other innovations have lowered the costs and expanded the potential formats for collective actions. It is possible that someone could have organized a large-scale flash mob in which hundreds of people arrived at the same place, at the same time, and danced the same dance via the postal service. But it is a lot faster, cheaper, and more plausible with GPS-enabled mobile phones, YouTube how-to videos, and social media. The same applies to social movements. When Ayatollah Khomeini was exiled in Paris, his speeches inciting revolution in Iran were spread via cassette tapes that were copied one by one and passed covertly from person to person. Today, his counterparts would post videos on YouTube, where they are easily and instantly accessible to a global audience.

Social Movements and Innovation in Organizations

But what does this have to do with business? Mayer Zald, our mentor and friend, pointed out in the late 1970s that social movements happen in organizations much as they do in society—including *coups d'état,* insurgencies, and mass movements.[5] In some sense, most large organizations look a lot like nation-states, with leaders, hierarchies, borders, and sometimes air forces. Some kinds of social movements in organizations are obvious, such as efforts to establish labor unions. But there are notable others:

- **Coup d'état:** Morgan Stanley's merger with Dean Witter Discover in 1997 had left ongoing tensions between legacy employees. Partisans of the old Morgan Stanley, many of them no longer with the company, agitated to oust CEO Philip Purcell, who had originally come from Dean Witter and sought to implement reforms that went against the white-shoe culture of the old-school investment bank. He was ultimately fired and replaced with John Mack, a Morgan Stanley favorite.[6]

- **Insurgency:** At HealthSouth, the campaign against CEO Richard Scrushy was more like an insurgency, with disgruntled employees sharing evidence of fraud on the Yahoo Finance electronic bulletin board. Although early members of the insurgency were punished, Scrushy was ultimately convicted in civil court and did prison time on an unrelated offense.[7]

- **Mass movement:** We also see grassroots initiatives in organizations that look more like traditional social movements such as the civil rights movement. During the 1990s, informal employee groups at dozens of American corporations organized to press for domestic partner benefits, typically insurance coverage for partners of LGBT employees equivalent to that available to spouses of straight employees. What began as a radical idea embraced by a handful of high-tech companies such as Lotus spread and was ultimately embraced by the Big Three automakers—with the support of the United Auto Workers. In 2013, even Walmart announced the adoption of domestic partner benefits.[8]

Most importantly for the purpose of social intrapreneurs, innovations often emerge through social movements. While we do not expect top executives to applaud corporate coups or insurgencies, they may be more amenable to internal social movements because these can be a source of innovation that keeps the organization better attuned to a rapidly changing environment.

Many things that we take for granted today, from women's right to vote to the organic food sold at Walmart, came out of social movements. Some entailed challenges to authority and civil disobedience (e.g., India's independence from its cruel and hated British oppressors); others required a widespread change of attitudes in the population (e.g., the gay rights movement).

In our conversations with intrapreneurs, we found a consistent theme: championing an innovation was like leading a social movement. The content often varied—from adopting green practices in the office to creating a triple-bottom-line product offering to sourcing raw materials from farmers in low-income countries like Rwanda—but the processes resembled each other.

One of our favorite intrapreneurs is Kevin Thompson at IBM. Although Thompson's post-MBA position at IBM did not include the title "Social Intrapreneur," his idea for a corporate Peace Corps at Big Blue required the skills of an activist to get off the ground. What was the right time? IBM CEO Sam Palmisano had launched an effort to be a "globally integrated enterprise" in 2006. Yet because the company's workforce was increasingly dispersed around the world, the kind of face-to-face collaboration that generates innovation and strong ties was potentially limited. Moreover, global companies were increasingly being called on to earn their "license to operate" by demonstrating their social value. As Thompson tells it, "The big signal for us was the chairman's piece on the globally integrated enterprise in *Foreign Affairs* magazine."[9] This was the opportunity to advocate for an initiative that would bring IBM's resources to bear on addressing social problems in low-income countries.

Why a corporate Peace Corps? Because it provided boots-on-the-ground experience solving problems in resource-constrained environments, often in countries that IBM had yet to serve. It is more effective to acquire a global mind-set working with colleagues in a village in Ghana than in an air-conditioned hotel in London. Moreover, it was far, far cheaper. The connections generated in this context, both within and beyond IBM, would be of great value.

Who were the right allies? Given that the central business benefit to IBM was in leadership development, potential sponsors and allies were largely in the human resources function. As alumni of the program came home, they helped create a web of allies across the company and around the world, helping to ensure that the program would live beyond the pilot stage.

Most organizations do not lack for innovative ideas. The gap is in bringing them to fruition. Nokia had internal plans for smartphones and tablets with many of the features credited to the iPhone—several years before Apple's products made their appearance.[10] But corporate politics and the allure of easy profits from traditional phones prevented Nokia from taking their innovations to market. Similarly, many companies have the makings of leading-edge social innovations within their borders. They simply don't have processes in place to nurture the good ones and bypass the less-good ones.

As we will show in chapter 8, companies can benefit from creating a culture of social innovation that enables such movements. That doesn't mean that every innovation that comes down the pike should be pursued. Most mutations are a bad idea. But failing to allow good ones to develop can leave the company blindsided by changes in the environment. It is better to learn about human rights issues in the supply chain from internal advocates than from a consumer boycott.

Opportunities: When Is the Time Ripe for Change?

Innovations can be before or after their time. Those over forty may remember the Apple Newton, a '90s-era harbinger of mobile computing, complete with (highly imperfect) handwriting recognition. Early on in his second tenure at Apple, Steve Jobs killed the Newton, to the lamentations of its (modest-sized) fan base. Ubiquitous Wi-Fi, low-cost color touchscreens, and other elements that make the smartphone what it is simply were not in place yet to make the Newton a hit. Similarly, not every company may be ready for carbon tracking at the same time.

Survey the Landscape

Introducing a movement or innovation appropriately requires first knowing the *terrain*—the relatively slow-changing parts of the landscape. In a company, these are the strategy, structure, and culture. They can often be identified through corporate documents and filings that help provide a terrain map of the organization.

- *Strategy* describes the set of decisions that map the organization's path forward. It includes answers to a few core questions: What is our mission? What are our markets, and how do we serve them in a distinctive way? What is our industry like? How do we assess our performance? It is exceedingly difficult to champion an innovation that does not align with the organization's strategy; thus, knowing the strategy and the means the company is using to pursue it is critical for social intrapreneurs. Fortunately, it takes only modest effort to uncover a company's strategy, particularly if it is a public corporation. (Perhaps surprisingly, research suggests that the large majority of employees have little idea what their company's stated strategy is, even when presented with a multiple-choice option!)

- *Structure* refers to the organization's formal design, including the organization chart and reporting relations, compensation systems, evaluation processes, and other formalized means used to guide action in support of the strategy.

- *Culture* expresses the mental model that provides coherence to the organization's actions. Culture is displayed through things like the language people use, the stories they tell, the dress code and style that prevails, and the physical space in which people work. Underlying this is a set of ideas about how the organization should operate, which sets some parameters for innovation. Although knowing a culture thoroughly could take years of intensive fieldwork, software tools can provide a useful shortcut for diagnosing the culture.

Know When to Make Your Move

The second element to take note of when considering an innovation is the *timing*—those things that change more rapidly and that are particularly prone to signaling opportunities. This includes the business environment and the actions of competitors, changing customer demands, and internal changes such as leadership that make the time more or less welcoming for an innovation.

Leadership changes often signal opportunities. New CEOs arrive with new priorities and new programs, and social innovations often find an opening here. Although still in his thirties, Justin DeKoszmovszky has been a change agent across several large and growing consumer packaged goods firms. When speaking in our MBA class on intrapreneurship, his easy manner, dry wit, and charming humility endear him to our students right away. For MBA students wanting to make a positive difference in the world, DeKoszmovszky is like the big brother they wish they had had when growing up in large organizations. The students latch onto his perspective quickly, recognizing that they could soon be following in his footsteps. DeKoszmovszky told us that at SC Johnson, "Major points of inflection or change—new products, jobs, public reports, and so on—are the biggest opportunities in terms of timing."

Changes in what competitors are doing can also be an opportunity, particularly when they alter the prospects for recruiting. The actions of other organizations provide a useful rhetorical resource: "If X is greening its supply chain, do we really want to be left behind?"

Timing an innovation also depends on your own career stage. A new manager fresh from an MBA program who arrives with a dozen great ideas to shake the place up is unlikely to be welcomed. Getting to know the lay of the land and developing a few allies—preferably, at least some of them senior—are essential steps to being able to lead a major social innovation effectively. Gib Bulloch explained that he had been at Accenture for roughly five years before founding the Accenture Development Partnerships program. During that time, he came to know the culture, built up his professional network and credibility, learned who were potential allies (or not), and understood which rules were hard constraints.

In chapter 4, we provide tools to understand your company's strategy, structure, and culture to better connect your innovation to the company's priorities.

Framing: How Will You Convince Potential Allies and Decision Makers of the Value of Your Innovation?

The way an idea is presented, or framed, can strongly shape how it is received. *Frames* are the shared definitions and meanings people bring to a situation. A skilled intrapreneur can choose a frame in a way that predisposes his or her audience to buy it. An even more skilled intrapreneur can tailor the pitch to different audiences, while maintaining a core consistency.

An effective frame connects the innovation to the enduring values and priorities of the organization. Part of the opportunity structure is the company's culture—the DNA behind its choices. Innovations are often framed as solutions to a problem that the business faces. Different kinds of cultures are receptive to different kinds of frames, and therefore different frames are likely to be called for in a family business, an industrial business, or a market-oriented business. An intrapreneur we spoke to at a family-controlled business noted the value of emphasizing family imagery and legacy. But in more standard corporate settings, allusions to the latest article in *Harvard Business Review* seemed to have an almost hypnotic effect. Different cultures call for different frames.

Choosing the right vehicle to convey the innovation also helps. While PowerPoint presentations are the coin of the realm in business, innovations are often best conveyed through stories and images. The vivid story of a program's beneficiary can sometimes melt even the iciest CEO's heart. Yet even the best story must ultimately be backed up by a plausible business case. As corporate change agent Joe Malcoun—Joe was a consultant for a sustainability management firm called GreenOrder and then an intrapreneur himself at DTE Energy—emphasized, "The first conversation is the high-level business case. Can't have the other conversations until that is done. It must align with one of the corporate goals."

In chapter 5, we describe elements of effective frames and stories to convey them. We also provide a guide to linking the right kind of pitch to the organization's culture.

Networks: Who Are the Right People to Get Involved in Developing and Promoting Your Innovation?

Innovations spread faster when they are conveyed by the right people with the right set of connections. Even a highly contagious innovation will flounder if it only circulates in the periphery. To become widely accepted, particularly among the right allies, it helps to understand the networks in an organization. Malcolm Gladwell refers to three types of people who are especially useful in getting an innovation widely adopted: *mavens* (those whom others go to for advice); *connectors* (well-networked individuals who cross social boundaries); and *salespeople* (those who are particularly effective at persuading other people to adopt or support an innovation).[11] (There will be more on these types in chapter 6.)

Social network analysis is a great method for identifying the most relevant people to join your movement and the shortest paths to reach them. It has spawned software tools for measuring and visualizing social networks within and beyond organizations. Many of the terms used to describe participants in movements—such as *maven* or *connector*—correspond to the mathematical measures used in social network analysis.

The data necessary for social network analysis is increasingly available through sites like LinkedIn and through less obtrusive sources. Indeed, the US National Security Agency (NSA) has discovered that metadata from phone calls—who calls whom, and for how long—can be used to map out large-scale social structures.

Even without formal analysis of network data, skilled intrapreneurs are good at building and working their networks. Although it's helpful to be able to visualize the distance connecting innovators to decision makers (geodesics) or to calculate the network power of key players (eigenvector centralities), sometimes it is sufficient to ask "Does anybody know this guy, or know somebody who's worked with him that could give us some intel?" In the corporate world, we are rarely more than three degrees of separation away from those who can help or hinder us.

Chapter 6 provides a detailed guide to understanding networks, getting data, and analyzing it to map the social terrain of the organization.

Mobilizing: What Systems and Tools Can Help Organize for Action in This Situation?

The fourth element of our framework is the platforms or forums that can be used to collaborate. In the literature on movements, these are "mobilizing structures." For instance, the civil rights movement was greatly facilitated by the structure of African American churches in the South and elsewhere. They provided a place where large groups met regularly in a shared space. Moreover, individual churches were connected with each other through more or less formal channels.[12]

The ability to communicate and coordinate with allies allows the group to convey more effectively that they speak with a unified voice. The right platform can also enable the spread of information, tactics, and best practices. This was highlighted during the Arab Spring, where activists across countries shared ideas on Facebook, among other places. Some of it was concrete and tactical; for instance, that dipping a bandanna in vinegar was an effective method of filtering out tear gas. Some of it was at the level of principles and broad strategy; for instance, the broad benefits of seizing the moral high ground via nonviolence.[13]

Some kinds of mobilizing platforms make certain forms of organizing cheaper or more feasible. Scholars of human-computer interaction refer to a technology's *affordances*, features that make certain actions easier to see and do. Text messaging is an effective way to get brief snippets of information out to a small group of acquaintances. Facebook allows people to share pictures, links, and longer stories with approved others—if they have access to the Web. YouTube allows conveying vivid how-to information or sharing eyewitness accounts. BlackBerry has BBM, enabling encrypted messages that facilitated mass looting in the United Kingdom.

Those from the pre-internet days may recall participating in "phone trees" to convey pressing information. Each participant had the names and phone numbers of a small group of others whom they would call to share information. These people in turn had their own lists of names and numbers to call. Over the course of a couple of hours, it would be possible to reach hundreds of people. Of course, today such information could be shared instantly via Twitter. As a result, pressing information and calls to action are much more plausible.

One of the limitations of platforms such as Facebook in a corporate setting is that many large companies maintain tight limits on what kinds of software they allow access to. This was driven home to us when we sought to Skype with one of the guest intrapreneurs in our MBA class. At his company, employees were forbidden to install Skype or similar software on corporate computers, and the corporate Wi-Fi network made it impossible to connect via Skype. Our informant ended up borrowing a colleague's laptop, leaving the office, and Skyping us from a nearby coffeehouse that had Wi-Fi.

This incident highlighted that corporations typically have much tighter control over their internal communications network than the average authoritarian regime in the Middle East. Indeed, the software available for IT departments in companies to monitor e-mails and other communication puts the NSA to shame. This highlights that intrapreneurship is not without its hazards.

On the other hand, just about anyone can manage to evade the constraints of corporate IT systems by using a personal smartphone on a cellular network. The familiar meetings marked by under-the-table texting and knowing glances of those under thirty make those of us over forty feel like some kind of Kabuki theater is being played out. If the trend toward BYOD (bring your own device) in workplaces continues, the corporate IT department may no longer be in a position to play Big Brother.

In chapter 6, we describe some of the methods of collaboration and their affordances that enable social intrapreneurs to build momentum for their initiatives. We also note some of the hazards and limitations of these methods in a corporate setting.

CHAPTER FOUR

When: Opportunity Structures

Innovations and movements take hold at some times and places and not others. Wheeled luggage is ubiquitous among travelers today. What could be more obvious than putting wheels on a heavy suitcase? Yet the first patent for a wheeled suitcase was issued in 1972, and almost no one bought them until the Rollaboard was invented in 1987. Even then, it was initially aimed at airline crews and only later adopted by the general public.[1] Why did something so obvious take so long? Apparently, real men carried their bags—and real women rented carts— something that seems ludicrous today. In this mystery lies the secret of finding the right time for instigating change.

This chapter describes how you can assess your organization to understand what kinds of initiatives are likely to be feasible, as well as signals for the right time to pitch them. Our intrapreneurs emphasized that social innovations have to fit with the strategy, structure, and culture of the organization to get off the ground, no matter how worthy they might appear. Yet surprisingly few people can convey their company's strategy effectively or connect their innovation with the company's priorities like an insider. Similarly, insiders are particularly well suited to detect the best time to introduce an innovation, since this depends on what else is going on in the organization at that time and not just the nature of the innovation itself.

The civil rights movement in the United States became a powerful social movement in the 1950s, yet African Americans had experienced systematic oppression for generations before that, long after the post–Civil War reforms. What made the difference? One of the more surprising influences was the Cold War. Flagrant racial discrimination in the United States, including segregated armed forces, was a powerful propaganda tool for the Soviets as the global South decolonized: the Soviets could point to the hypocrisy of America's treatment of its own non-white citizens when wooing potential allies in Africa and elsewhere. Encouraged by the State Department and others, President Harry S. Truman set in motion a set of federal policies—starting with the President's Committee on Civil Rights in 1946 and highlighted by his 1948 executive order to desegregate the military—that created new prospects for progress in dismantling America's apartheid system.[2]

Authoritarian regimes reigned for decades in the Middle East with little effective organized resistance; yet in a few months in 2011, several fell like dominoes, including Egypt, the largest Arab country. Why then and not before? One hint came from a whimsical feature published in *The Economist* shortly after the beginning of unrest in Egypt called "the shoe-thrower's index," which yields a score for the potential for unrest in a Middle Eastern country in the near future. It combines a number of indicators believed to feed unrest, weighting each according to their importance, and adding them up. The most important factor is the proportion of the population under age twenty-five (that is, those most prone to street-level activism); next are years the government has been in power, level of corruption, level of lack of democracy, and so on. High scores match the places that experienced the Arab Spring surprisingly well.[3] Yet five years earlier, these factors would not have indicated "near-term unrest" at all. And perhaps now, four years later as we write this, they no longer do either. What was different then?

When Walmart—America's largest employer by far—began to offer domestic partner benefits in 2013, the practice was so common that it received little attention. According to a leaked internal memo, the decision was "a business decision, not a moral or political decision . . . Given the diverse world we live in today, a comprehensive benefit package that includes domestic partner benefits appeals to the contemporary workforce. Many companies, including most of our competitors, already offer spouse/partner benefits to their employees. Of thirty retail competitors, all but two (Publix and Stop & Shop union plan) provide either same- or opposite-sex domestic partner coverage."[4] What had changed?

We can imagine a shoe-thrower's index for an organization to measure the degree of readiness for innovations. It might include a handful of factors. One would be executive tenure: change is more likely during the early period of top executives' reigns, when new policies and directions are expected, or toward the end, when the executive is mindful of the legacy he or she will leave behind. A second would be workforce demographics. Millennials often have different priorities and expectations than baby boomers, so a relatively young workforce might imply openness to innovation, either arising from within a young workforce or in an effort to attract millennials. Recent organizational performance can also be a spur to social innovation. Research finds that problems in performance relative to competitors can promote a search for innovation, creating a potentially fruitful milieu for internal innovators. Paradoxically, a top executive at a publicly traded company recently confided to us that he is much more willing to *announce* increased investments being made into socially beneficial initiatives to investors when the financial performance of the company as a whole is looking especially strong.

Understanding the Opportunity Structure

Opportunity structure describes the situation in and around an organization that makes it the right time and place for an innovation or movement. The central questions we ask about opportunity structures are: Why do social movements arise when they do? What makes a social system receptive to change? What makes a social movement successful? and, What is the equivalent set of circumstances inside an organization? To answer these questions, intrapreneurs must first map the *terrain* for an innovation, then analyze the *timing* that makes an innovation more likely to be well received.

Imagine that you wanted to plan a picnic for your department in the next few weeks. Two of the key variables to think about are *where* it should be, which depends on the terrain, and *when,* which depends on what the weather is likely to be. Much the same is true about opportunities for innovation: it makes sense to plan for both the terrain and the timing.

Terrain describes the relatively long-lasting features of the company's landscape. This includes the company's strategy, structure, and culture. Timing, like the weather, is more changeable. Events in the business environment, personnel movements, developments in technology, mergers—any of these might affect the opportunity for an innovation. Effective intrapreneurship entails matching the innovation to the terrain and timing. In the rest of this chapter, we describe how to better understand each of these elements in your organization.

Terrain

The terrain creates limits on what is plausible as an innovation. Not all things that would improve the world are possible—companies have to make choices. A comparison of two seemingly similar initiatives is a good illustration.

One of Cascade Engineering's initiatives—pink recycling carts—threw us a bit at first. In 2012, our MBA students had prepared a beautiful chart mapping the relevance of Cascade's business units and social impact programs relative to the company's core business. Following conventional business school logic of "focus, focus, focus!", the students proudly unveiled the chart to CEO Fred Keller and his top team, who had joined us for the day. The recommendation the four students made was to step back from the pink cart business. Presentation over, the students waited eagerly for affirmation.

But the students had misunderstood the basis of decision making used by Keller, who, as we mentioned in chapter 2, followed the motto "Do all the good you can, By all the means you can, In all the ways you can, In all the places you can, At all the times you can, To all the people you can, As long as ever you can." The pink carts were advocated by JoAnne Perkins, a Cascade vice president and business unit leader, were wanted to help raise awareness of breast cancer. The carts were large and undeniably drew attention to Cascade's commitment to this cause. But how did they fit with Cascade's strategy and culture as a whole? When delicately asked, Keller was surprised at the question: the carts signified the company's commitment to a triple bottom line and, moreover, its openness to innovations from all employees. From his perspective, as well as being financially viable, the pink cart business was entirely consistent with the company's strategy. How could a campaign aimed at enhancing public health be inconsistent with any company's strategy? Keller feels that if something is good to do and it doesn't cost much, why would you *not* do it? This is a very different perspective than starting at the top of a list of projects prioritized by ROI.

On the other hand, when KFC introduced its "pink buckets" in 2010—donating 50 cents to the Susan G. Komen for the Cure foundation for every bucket of chicken sold—critics cried "fowl," not-so-gently pointing out the link between dietary fat, obesity, and the risk of cancer. Few would mistake KFC for a health-conscious organization, and public perceptions of this innovation were at best skeptical, and at worst scathing. The campaign did not return the following year.[5]

Some constraints are not quite as obvious, but equally powerful. Intrapreneurs at many consumer packaged goods (CPG) companies and retailers whom we have spoken to seek ways to reduce the supply chain's carbon footprint by reducing packaging and shipping weight. A seemingly obvious green innovation for products like laundry detergent is to make the product more concentrated, which results in smaller packages and lower weight, with no decline in the product's effectiveness—a win all around. Yet CPG firms battle ferociously for retail shelf space, which influences purchases at the point of sale. As long as the other guys continue to have monster-sized "economy" packaging, the would-be green competitor faces a dilemma.

Strategy

Strategy is the set of decisions that chart the organization's path forward. Strategy is not just a set of initiatives; it provides a multi-year sense of where the organization is headed and the broad steps it will take to get there. Why should intrapreneurs be steeped in the broader strategy of a company? Because it conveys credibility and seriousness of purpose. As Joe Malcoun told us, "You have to pick up the language of the company. Send the message that you are an insider." Having been part of a team consulting to General Electric on the start-up of its Ecomagination program, and as an internal consultant at DTE Energy, Malcoun would know: conveying a clear understanding of strategy is the place to start.

Strategy addresses a set of essential questions:

- What is our core mission? That is, why does this organization exist?

- What are our markets? Who are the constituencies we aim to serve?

- What is our industry like? Here, the standard method of analysis is Michael Porter's five forces model of the major features of industry competition: (1) buyer power, (2) supplier power, (3) existence of substitutes, (4) barriers to entry, and (5) the nature of competition.

- How do we serve our markets? What are our competencies? What tactics do we use to compete?

- How do we measure our (social and economic) performance?

For public companies—which includes almost all of the largest corporations in the United States—EDGAR provides an easy entry into understanding a company's strategy. EDGAR is the US Securities and Exchange Commission's Electronic Data Gathering, Analysis, and Retrieval database. It provides an electronic repository of essentially all documents that public companies, mutual funds, and a few other organizations are required to file.[6] It went live around 1994 and has been accumulating information ever since.

Suppose you were considering a job at Apple and wanted to know more about the company's strategy and your chances for leading a social initiative there. What should you look for? First, go to the EDGAR website and search for "AAPL" (Apple's ticker symbol). Two types of filings are most useful here, the annual report and the proxy statement. The annual report, or more specifically form 10-K, describes the state of the company's finances and its performance over the previous year, along with other useful information such as the number of employees, which countries the firm operates in, who its biggest shareholders are, and more. The proxy statement, DEF 14A, is mailed to shareholders each year to allow them to vote by proxy at the annual meeting. The proxy describes the company's board of directors, top officers, major shareholders, and gives a glimpse of how it defines performance. It also includes any shareholder resolutions proposed by activists outside the company.

Apple's 10-K provides a particularly clear statement of its strategy, major product lines, and priorities:

> *The Company is committed to bringing the best user experience to its customers through its innovative hardware, software and services. The Company's business strategy leverages its unique ability to design and develop its own operating systems, hardware, application software, and services to provide its customers new products and solutions with superior ease-of-use, seamless integration, and innovative design. The Company believes continual investment in research and development, marketing and advertising is critical to the development and sale of innovative products and technologies.*[7]

It also describes Apple's competitive landscape in terms amenable to a five forces analysis: its markets/customers and how concentrated they are; the nature of its competition; the character of its component suppliers; barriers to entry from patents, trademarks, and copyrights; and other details.

Companies are also required to describe in some detail the risks they face. Thanks to the influence of lawyers, these are surprisingly frank:

- "There can be no assurance the Company will be able to continue to provide products and services that compete effectively."

- "The financial condition of these resellers could weaken, these resellers could stop distributing the Company's products, or uncertainty regarding demand for the Company's products could cause resellers to reduce their ordering and marketing of the Company's products."

- "There can be no assurance the Company will be able to detect and fix all defects in the hardware, software and services it sells. Failure to do so could result in lost revenue, significant warranty and other expenses, and harm to the Company's reputation."

- "The Company's business may be impacted by political events, war, terrorism, public health issues, natural disasters and other circumstances."[8]

In fact, Apple lists more than two dozen separate significant risk factors, seemingly designed to scare away all but the hardiest investors. Some of these provide a virtual menu of potential problems for innovators to solve.

The remainder of the report includes detailed financial data, broken down by product segment and geography. You can learn how many employees the company has in what segments, what countries are responsible for most of its revenues and profits, which segments are growing fastest, and more. From downloading just one file, it is possible to get an excellent view of the company's industry, strategy, and priorities, which will be invaluable in helping guide efforts at intrapreneurship.

Now imagine you want to know more about Pfizer before starting your summer internship. What can you learn from its proxy statement? Early on, Pfizer gives clear information about its priorities and performance. It describes four "imperatives" put into place in early 2011:

- Improving the Performance of our Innovative Core

- Making the Right Capital Allocation Decisions

- Earning Greater Respect from Society

- Creating a Culture of Ownership[9]

Already, the social innovator is noting the encouragement contained in the third imperative ("Earning Greater Respect from Society").

Pfizer also described its performance in terms of key indicators:

> *We brought five new therapies to patients for treating kidney cancer, leukemia, rheumatoid arthritis, stroke prevention in atrial fibrillation, and the rare Gaucher disease. We also drove solid revenue growth in many of our key, patent-protected products and achieved double-digit revenue growth in emerging markets. Despite an industry record $7.4 billion operational loss in sales due to patent expirations, we maintained relatively flat adjusted earnings per share and we returned nearly $15 billion to shareholders through dividends and share repurchases.*[10]

Finally, it describes its "Executive compensation philosophy, goals, and actions," providing insight into what key executives get rewarded for at Pfizer—knowledge of which is quite useful when thinking through what kinds of initiatives are going to be easy to pitch, and which ones are going to be an uphill battle.

Next are short biographies of the directors and a set of brief reports from various board committees, further highlighting some of the company's priorities. The value of this information is that it gives clues to directors' backgrounds, interests, and likely receptivity to different kinds of initiatives. If a director is also on the board of MoveOn.org, it is unlikely that he or she will support "Concealed-Carry Friday." We also learn that BlackRock is Pfizer's largest shareholder, and the only one that owns more than 5 percent of its shares—something Pfizer has in common with several hundred other large companies.

A detailed section on executive compensation provides further detail on performance and the "four imperatives." The expiration of Pfizer's patent on Lipitor, its highly lucrative cholesterol drug, along with other expirations, led to a 14 percent decline in US revenues. New initiatives for charitable contributions might not face the most welcoming environment this year.

We learn that the chief initiatives under "earning greater respect from society" included a program aimed at creating broad dialogues around successful aging and another program to provide underinsured patients access to low- or no-cost medicines. This provides further useful information on what kinds of innovations are likely to find an audience at Pfizer.

Structure

Structure describes the organization's design: the processes, reporting relations, compensation system, and other formalized methods used to pursue the organization's strategy. A central purpose of understanding the organization's structure is to map who is at the table in key decisions.

The simplest starting point is the organization chart and associated lists of responsibilities. Some of these positions are easy to track down—for instance, who is on the board of directors, who serves legally as an "officer" of the organization, who heads a particular division or department. Relatively senior people often have available biosketches that give some sense of their interests and outside ties. Executives are often invited to give speeches and participate on panels at conferences, which typically entails providing a brief biography that might describe their career history and current activities, such as what nonprofit boards they serve on. Much of this information is also readily available online. All these sources can give a better sense of what the organization's higher-ups value and what kinds of initiatives they are likely to support.

Unfortunately, these executives are often at a high enough level that you are not likely to encounter them personally. A serial intrapreneur who worked at a global CPG company told us that while there was great support at the top levels of the company for social innovation, "The challenge is every level below that." We think of this as a "missing middle" of leading change in organizations. Top management and idealistic millennials often have a broader vision of the system than the middle managers locked in by golden handcuffs and financial incentives. In navigating the complexity of a large corporation, even personal acquaintance with the CEO was no guarantee of success.

How to get to know the immediate structure? Katharine Bierce, one energetic intrapreneur we spoke with, described a more immediately useful method of getting to know the organization's structure and key people that is particularly useful for new recruits. First, print out the "About Us" section of the web page, which commonly includes photos and some biographical information. Do a little research to find out something about each person. Bierce used announcements of new hires and the company intranet to find like-minded colleagues in her home office and around the world. (If your organization doesn't have an intranet, Google is sufficient—you don't need to examine your potential allies' credit scores.) Based on their jobs and backgrounds, find something useful you might be able to provide them, such as a problem you might be able to solve or a connection you might be able to make. Then, make a point of introducing yourself when the time arises and, if appropriate, offering your help: "I understand you are working with a children's literacy organization. Are they looking for volunteers?" "Actually, I worked with marketing strategy in my last job, if you need another pair of eyes to look over your outreach plan . . ." Last, if you have an option of where to locate your desk, avoid the temptation to find a window seat. "Sit near a printer and you'll get to know everyone!" says Bierce. In organizational reality, the "elevator pitch" is just as much about making a credible personal connection as it is selling an idea in sixty seconds. A favorable first impression opens the door to further consideration with a more reasonable discussion window than a six-floor journey in a steel box.

Culture

Culture is the mental model or "theory of the business" that holds the organization together. Peter Drucker described it as the source from which other parts of the organization spring.[11] Culture often reflects the priorities of the founder(s), and in family businesses, core values can live on for generations. Unlike strategy, culture is not always written down in securities filings.

In his classic *Organizational Culture and Leadership*, MIT's Edgar Schein describes the central questions and assumptions that underlie culture:[12]

- **The organization's relationship to its environment:** What business are we in? Who are our major constituencies?

- **The nature of reality and truth:** How are "facts" determined? How do we make decisions?

- **The nature of human nature:** Are people fundamentally good or bad, fixed or changeable?

- **The nature of human activity:** What are the "right" things for people to do? What is the best way to influence or control human action?

- **The nature of human relationships:** How should people relate to each other—cooperation or competition, individualism or collaboration?

These assumptions are revealed in visible aspects of the organization that often strike visitors almost immediately:

- The *language* used to communicate assumptions, values, and ideologies of the organization. At one large retailer we studied, for instance, inclusion and diversity are widely used terms expressing one of the company's central values. Extending beyond gender and ethnic diversity into programs for other forms of inclusion—diversity of ideas and openness to dissent—was an elegant and effective bridge.

- *Artifacts or props* used to reinforce values and ideology. At Leo Burnett, the Chicago-based advertising agency, the ubiquitous thick pencils and bowls of apples convey the founder's values of creativity and integrity.

- *Stories and jargon* used to draw attention to norms and heroes or role models. Shortly after William Clay "Bill" Ford Jr. took over as chairman of Ford Motor Company, an explosion and fire struck its aging River Rouge plant, a short distance from Ford's world headquarters. Mr. Ford was advised against heading to the scene, which was still volatile, and was told that generals don't go to the front lines. His response: "Bust me down to private then, because I'm out of here." A visibly emotional Ford spoke to employees and the press at the scene: "Everyone who works for Ford is an extended member of the family. This is the worst day of my life." His words conveyed that Ford is a family business, with all that it implies.

- *Dress or uniform* used to establish positive organizational identity. At Whole Foods, the diversity of dress, piercings, tattoos, and hairstyles signals a defiantly un-uniform approach to management and an openness to new thinking.

- *Physical settings and surroundings* can create an environment that reinforces values. At Cascade Engineering, the corporate headquarters is housed in Michigan's first LEED-EB (Leadership in Energy and Environmental Design Existing Building) Platinum–certified building. The "Learning Center"—a signal of company's triple-bottom-line commitment.

To get at all of these elements could take the training of a cultural anthropologist and years of fieldwork. Fortunately, there are some tools that can help provide a shortcut to diagnosing an organization's culture through content analysis of its documents.

Content analysis is a fancy term for describing computerized coding of a body of text. The most straightforward kind of content analysis is simply to count the number of times a particular word or phrase occurs in a text. (Free online software exists for this.[13]) The basic idea is that the frequency of the occurrence of words and phrases tells us something about their importance to the person or organization that uses them. This is the theory behind the now-ubiquitous word cloud diagrams that connect the size of the word to its frequency.

Suppose you counted the frequency of all two-word phrases in Apple's description of risk factors in its annual report. What turns up—what is Apple worried about? In addition to not-too-meaningful phrases like "of the," "in the," and "subject to," we see "third party," "intellectual property," "new products," "operating results," and "trade receivables."

Content analysis becomes particularly useful if the prevalence of words and phrases can be used to diagnose the culture. Klaus Weber at Northwestern University has compiled a very helpful dictionary of terms associated with different kinds of corporate cultures. Weber's theory is that the kind of vocabulary a company routinely uses reveals which of several broad kinds of cultural orientations an organization follows. He describes seven generic types of culture (see table 4-1).[14] By matching the kinds of terminology used in corporate documents with the dictionary, it is possible to get an initial sense of what kind of culture we are dealing with, and therefore what initiatives are plausible (and how they might be pitched, which we describe in the next chapter).

Where does one get the documents to analyze? Corporate financial documents, letters to shareholders, speeches by executives, and more are readily available online in most cases. The general rule is, the more the merrier: the larger and more varied the corpus, the greater the confidence that the results are not the idiosyncratic characteristics of a particular kind of document (EBITDA turns up much more often in the 10-K than in corporate environmental reports, for instance).

A particularly useful source of information about corporate culture is recruiting documents and websites. It is here that

TABLE 4-1

Types of corporate culture and associated management logics

Logic	Organization metaphor	Basis of evaluation; source of personal status	Decision criteria; conflict resolution	Exemplary organizations
Inspired	Religious group	*Inspiration:* Enthusiasm, genius, ability to create excitement (e.g., charismatic leaders)	Vision, imagination, intuition, creativity, gut feel, lived experience, calling	Churches, value-driven enterprises, "hot" R&D teams
Family	Household	*Tradition:* Seniority, trust, virtue, solidarity, harmony, wisdom (e.g., patriarchic leaders)	Etiquette, conventions and manners, duty, respect of rank and hierarchy	Family enterprises, "traditional" Japanese companies, military units
Popularity	Flash mob	*Popularity:* Visibility, fame, recognition, fashion, public opinion (e.g., stars, celebrity CEOs)	Opinion, surveys, majority view, campaigns, fashion	Fashion and entertainment firms
Civic	Democracy	*Common good:* Rules and responsibilities, unity, equality, and rights (e.g., elected leaders)	Participation, debate, equity, compromise, policies, procedures, delegation, voting	Community organizations, cooperatives, some partnerships (e.g., law, consulting)
Market	Marketplace	*Demand:* Customers, price, competition, success (e.g., highest paid/wealthy CEO)	Benchmarking with competition, return on investment, customer demand, contract	Investment banking, contractors, entrepreneurs
Industrial	Machine	*Efficiency:* Performance, functionality, expertise (e.g., technical expert/professional)	Measurement, analysis, data, planning, capacity, expert judgment	Engineering and process technology firms
Sustainable	Ecosystem	*Future sustenance:* Stakeholder benefits, responsibility, health of system (e.g., social entrepreneurs)	Resource "footprint," stewardship for others and future, natural, encompassing, system impact	Alternative agriculture, social enterprises, "green enterprises"

Source: Klaus Weber, "Converging Orders of Worth: Adaptive and Demographic Mechanisms of Cultural Globalization," Kellogg School of Management Technical Note, forthcoming.

companies aim most explicitly to convey their values to actual or potential employees. This is, in a sense, their "best self" on display. Google, for instance, lists "Ten things we know to be true" under "What we believe," including "Democracy on the web works" (#4), "You can make money without doing evil" (#6), and "You can be serious without a suit" (#9).[15]

Of course, the best self is not always the one we are likely to encounter on the ground. Internal memos are preferable to external documents to assess culture. A window into internal culture in Glassdoor.com, a website with reviews by current and former employees. There is, naturally, some bias here: on the one hand, the kinds of people who post might be true believers who love the company; on the other, they might be disgruntled former employees who want to vent. Taken together, however, the reviews can provide a surprisingly informative sense of what a company values in practice (compared with how it portrays itself to the outside world). And combining them with what content analysis of a company's own documents reveals is likely to give a strong sense of what is valued and how they talk about it.

Timing

Those who are mulling the best time to have children are sometimes advised that no time is ever really good. Attending school, starting a new job, taking on new responsibilities, looking after older parents—there is always a good reason to say "Maybe later," so . . . might as well dive in now. While we are sympathetic to this argument, it does not always apply in a corporate setting. Just as the weather changes over time, organizations experience changes in leadership, initiatives, competitor actions, and the broader social and economic environment. That means that there really are better and worse times to advocate for an initiative, even within the same organization. In this section, we describe some of the clues that signal that the time is right for introducing your social innovation.

Social movement researchers suggest three broad categories of political opportunity, each of which has analogues at the organizational level. Of course, these factors can tilt the playing field but are no guarantee of success. Moreover, each can introduce its own dangers, as we will describe.

How Open Is the Political System?

How open the political system is shapes how easy it is to advocate for innovation. Changes in openness make for changes in opportunity. In the case of the American civil rights movement, Truman's creation of the President's Committee on Civil Rights in late 1946, and his desegregation of the military in 1948, served notice that efforts at dismantling the American system of segregation had new allies and opportunities. Civil rights activism would not be fruitless.

What are the corporate equivalents?

- At Liberty Media, new CEO Gregory Maffei aimed to signal openness: "At Liberty, one executive challenges me more than everyone else. I respect his opinion enormously, but he's not always easy with his challenges. And he was the first guy I gave a promotion to. Two of the other executives came up and said to me, 'Well, if we knew beating up on you was the way to get promoted, we would have done it, too.'"[16]

- Bernard Tyson, CEO of Kaiser Permanente, has an American flag on his desk and tells people it symbolizes freedom of speech. He says, "Now, why would I ever want anyone to walk into my office and not exercise the freedom of speech? One of the things I am working extremely hard on is to create an environment of transparency and the freedom of speech. I tell people: 'You can say whatever you want to say in this office to me. Just understand that I also have the freedom not to agree, but I want to know what you're thinking. I want to know what's on your mind, because I want to make the best decision that's going to make this organization thrive.'"[17]

- At Bloomberg, the layout of the office, with the CEO in an open space right in the middle of the bull pen, made it clear that the CEO was open to ideas. Curtis Ravenal, an intrapreneur who advocated for putting ESG (environmental, social, and governance) metrics directly on the homepage of companies on the Bloomberg terminal, had a desk only a few feet away, making it a far more hospitable environment for innovation than some other places.[18]

- At Google, the "20 percent rule" that characterized the company for its first several years meant that employees were allowed and encouraged to spend 20 percent of their time working on their own pet projects and innovations. The formal recognition of this as legitimate activity also signaled openness of the system.

Conversely, we have often heard from the intrapreneurs we spoke with that social innovations are considered "extracurricular activity" that should be done on their own time—and if you have time, maybe you're not working hard enough on your "real" job. One described how a collaborator was approached by her manager and asked what she was working on. She replied "the green team project," which had been endorsed by the CEO. The manager said, "If you have time to work on that, I am clearly not giving you enough to do."

Frictions at the Top

Frictions at the top can create opportunities as well as dangers. In the wake of mergers and other realignments, there are sometimes splits between different contingents of executives. When Citicorp merged with Travelers Group, the power-sharing arrangement between John Reed and Sandy Weill—both long-standing leaders of their respective organizations— seemed ill-fated from the start, as the parts of each organization intended to produce synergies often produced conflicts. Investment bankers and commercial bankers often seem like different species, from how they deal with clients to how they are compensated, and (according to Reed) the investment banking culture came to dominate, with disastrous consequences when the financial crisis of 2008 arose.

This dynamic was even more pronounced after the Morgan Stanley merger with Dean Witter Discover in 1997. The cultural clash between the venerable white-shoe investment bank—which traced its lineage back to the House of Morgan—and the plebeian financial adviser most prominently linked to Sears, lasted for years. A power struggle between Phillip Purcell, who had been CEO of Dean Witter, and John Mack, CEO of Morgan Stanley, led to Mack's ouster in 2001.

Four years later, after a revolt by Morgan Stanley bankers and a public campaign by cadre of former executives, Purcell was out and Mack returned as CEO.

How can this divisive environment be an opportunity? Divergent views mean that there are alternative possibilities for the future of the firm, opening space for new initiatives. This is the corporate equivalent of knowing that if Dad says no, you can ask Mom and potentially get a different response. On the other hand, tensions such as these also signal that a lot of initiatives are likely to fall by the wayside when the smoke clears. For several years, Pfizer incubated the global Access to Medicines business unit with the goal of bringing medicine to low-income populations in developing countries in ways that were both affordable for the target markets and profitable for the company. Then, CEO Jeff Kindler was ousted in what was described by some commentators as a "palace coup," and succeeded by Ian Read.[19] As invariably happens in such situations, in a matter of months almost all of Kindler's appointees were replaced with his successor's men. Read seemingly had much less enthusiasm for longer-term, nontraditional investments, such as the global Access to Medicines initiative. Jean-Michel Halfon, the head of Emerging Markets at Pfizer, appeared to be one of the casualties of the leadership change. Halfon had championed the initiative. Within a few months of Halfon's departure, Access to Medicines was history and the work of a team of social intrapreneurs over several years was lost.

Elite Allies

Having elite allies—those who share values with the idea you are promoting—creates a more welcoming environment for pitching innovations. By most accounts, President Truman's background offered little reason to expect that he would be a friend of civil rights. Even his admiring biographer, Merle Miller, stated that he routinely expressed racist and anti-Semitic views, and he was briefly a member of the Ku Klux Klan.[20] Yet while in office, Truman's actions, if not his views, shifted to favor federal action in support of civil rights, to the consternation of Southern Democrats.

When William Clay "Bill" Ford Jr. took over as CEO of Ford Motor company in 2001, his history as an environmentalist signaled new opportunities for activists within the firm. At the time, Ford's profitable lineup of SUVs included the Excursion—described when it was introduced as the "biggest sport utility on the planet," and with gas mileage close to single digits. Yet Bill Ford's presence at the helm prompted a shift at the company favoring activism around the environment and more broadly.[21] Ford phased out the Excursion in 2005 and introduced an array of hybrid vehicles. Moreover, it became the first auto company to introduce a human rights code.

Ford's openness to internal social innovations was evidenced by its innovative program to combat HIV among employees and their families in South Africa, which had been recognized by the US State Department—a program initially championed by an intrapreneur within Ford. Upon accepting an award for Ford's HIV/AIDS programs from the Global Business Coalition in HIV/AIDS, Tuberculosis, and Malaria, Ford South Africa's CEO Jeff Nemeth stated, "Ford South Africa is like a family, and we look out for family."

The flip side is that having an elite sponsor can be precarious. Many initiatives supported by one CEO are summarily dropped by his or her successor.

Discrete Signals of Opportunity

Stanford's Doug McAdam has identified a number of smaller, discrete clues that signal the right time to suggest an innovation.[22] One sign of opportunity is when the company's espoused values and actual practices are visibly out of alignment. Of course, this happens to all organizations to some extent, unless their vision and values are unremarkable ("Incrementally increase EBITDA every year"). But events such as the elevation of a new CEO or the announcement of a new strategy or mission can be an opportunity to reexamine these disconnects. When Bill Ford announced that the company would improve the fuel efficiency of its SUVs by 25 percent, many in the company found it implausible—which, in fact, it was. But it created an entry point for those advocating alternative innovations that contributed to the company's green street cred.

The social intrapreneurs we spoke with pointed to major points of inflection in strategy, such as launches of new programs or major new products, as particularly ripe times for advocating innovation. These moments provide a natural opportunity to add features. For instance, the launch of a new type of sneaker aimed at millennials might be an apt time to push for introducing organic cotton or reducing the supply chain's carbon footprint, such as Puma's Clever Little Bag, a shoebox and bag in one designed to reduce packaging waste. Similarly, when two intrapreneurs we conversed with learned of their company's plans for building a large new facility, they saw it as a prime opportunity to use their influence. It is much easier and more cost effective to get sustainability built into the architecture during a planning phase than it is to try to change the design and materials after ground has been broken. The new building served as a rallying cry for interested social intrapreneurs throughout the whole company to coordinate and focus their efforts.

Sometimes particular events create grievances that provide an opening for innovators. Imagine an oil company that touts its commitment to the environment, yet is suddenly held responsible for a seemingly endless oil spill that despoils a vast coastline. Paradoxically, such a disjuncture between word and deed can create opportunities for internal innovators who point to a way to reduce the gap.

Some events dramatize the system's vulnerability. These events need not be in conflict with the organization's stated values, but they nonetheless create a moment for internal debate. As we saw in chapter 3, when the Susan G. Komen for the Cure foundation cut off funding for Planned Parenthood's cancer screenings for low-income women, it prompted an immediate nationwide backlash against the foundation and threats from tens of thousands of actual or potential supporters to withhold further contributions. Such an existential threat to an organization can also be an opportunity for internal activists who can propose innovative paths forward.

A final category of openings for social innovators comes from the actions of competitors. It is hard to overestimate the power of competitive benchmarking as a spur to action. Discovering that one's organization is below the industry median or failing to keep up with best practices is often a useful conversation starter, particularly as the recruiting season for MBAs approaches. No one wants to stand in front of a room full of potential recruits—particularly millennials—and explain why the company lacks a LEED-certified headquarters, or "dog at the office" policy, or 20 percent innovation time. We have been consistently impressed by the extent to which recruiting concerns provide an impetus to change corporate practice. The ability to point to diversity-friendly HR policies, carbon-minimizing facilities, and a rigorous record of upholding human rights throughout the supply chain is a competitive advantage in the war for talent. As Kevin Thompson told us, one of the many factors that helped the Corporate Service Corps gain traction at IBM was the fact that friends of the CEO's college-aged children thought it was really cool.

John Maynard Keynes famously said, "Worldly wisdom teaches that it is better for reputation to fail conventionally than to succeed unconventionally."[23] While on the surface this suggests that the deck is stacked against innovators, in many cases the opposite is true, because companies fear being industry laggards. Activists who advocated for domestic partner benefits in the 1990s were often highly aware of which other companies had adopted this practice; indeed, those we spoke to were often in contact with their counterparts in other companies, which allowed them to address wild fears among their own executives with concrete evidence of experience elsewhere. The programs were far less costly and controversial than skeptics feared and for some categories of potential employees, they were central concerns. Moreover, the more conventional the previous adopters, the stronger the case for going forward. As researchers Forrest Briscoe and Sean Safford discovered, when the Big Three automakers, in collaboration with the United Auto Workers union, adopted domestic partner benefits in 1999, it signaled that domestic partner benefits were as all-American as hot dogs, apple pie, and Chevrolet.[24] Briscoe and Safford labeled this the "Nixon-in-China effect," alluding to the fact that it took a staunch anti-Communist like Richard Nixon to be able to normalize diplomatic relations with China.[25]

A final piece of advice from successful intrapreneurs about getting the timing right is to do a feasibility check with trusted senior informants. There are always events in the company that are invisible below the senior executive level and that influence how hospitable the environment will be for innovations. Quietly checking with subject matter experts or others with access to senior levels can make clearer the feasibility of an initiative before expending too much energy on an endeavor that is likely to be futile.

Conclusion

We have argued that an innovator's success will be enhanced by understanding the context and timing the innovation appropriately. Think of it as "intrapreneurial aikido": using the movement of the system to help you execute your innovation. But remember that timing does not just depend on the company. It also depends on your own career stage.

It needn't be late in your career. As one of our interviewees, a senior leader at a large consulting firm, said when we asked him what he wished he had known when he started his career as an intrapreneur, "That I had the ability to shape the firm straight away. I didn't need to wait twenty years to do it. And I didn't need to leave the firm to find meaning." In some settings, such as professional service firms, we learned of many initiatives led by fairly junior people. At one consulting firm, a program to train talent to serve on nonprofit boards and to place them in organizations in their communities was championed by an associate only two years out of college. We heard many similar stories from consulting, accounting, and IT firms.

That said, the innovative ideas of the newly hired MBA, ready to leverage her core competence for disruptive Six Sigma sustainability, are not always welcomed warmly by colleagues who have been with the company for years. Although we have found that even interns can sometimes make a big difference, it's best to learn the lay of the land first and develop allies before sharing your bold insights too forcefully.

An important thing to recognize at the start is that both opportunities and good ideas to match them are plentiful. As they say in the Marines, when you are surrounded, it doesn't matter which direction you attack. Consider this: of all the ways Goldman Sachs could use its vast resources to address the world's problems, why is educating women entrepreneurs in low-income countries the right one? Certainly it is a worthy goal, but it is not the only possibility. Why is Pfizer pursuing successful aging? Why is Cascade Engineering making pink carts? *Because somebody made it happen.*

These examples suggest that a social innovator does well to take a portfolio approach—to have a variety of potential projects on tap and to pursue those that best fit with emerging conditions. Isaiah Berlin cited an ancient Greek poet for the claim that the fox knows many things, but the hedgehog knows one big thing.[26] We advise you to be a fox: the fox has many opportunities to pursue a change agenda; the hedgehog may have only one.

CHAPTER FIVE

Why: Making the Case

Social intrapreneurs often find themselves seeking to make a persuasive case for their innovation in a limited amount of time—the proverbial elevator pitch. Because elevators rarely have a projector for an impromptu PowerPoint presentation, the pitch must be short, engaging, relevant, and verbal. Like "A corporate Peace Corps to help create a globally integrated enterprise." Moreover, the pitch is most effective if it is customized for the audience at hand.

In this chapter, we provide some guidance on how to frame an innovation to give it the best chance to succeed. There are three elements to making the case for social innovations in organizations. First, as discussed in some depth in chapter 4, we must understand the culture of an organization and its context to diagnose what is possible. Second, we need to craft a frame that will engage potential allies but (ideally) not activate what Accenture's Gib Bulloch calls "the corporate antibodies" that seek to kill off anything that departs from the norm. Finally, we choose the right "vehicle" to convey the message. For many of our intrapreneurs, the vehicle often takes the form of a skillfully developed story.

Framing Battles

Framing battles are all around us. They take place within social movements and political movements as different sides aim to present things in their own way. Let's start by considering an example of a recent social change. In the spring of 2012, restaurant chains and grocery stores in the United States faced a massive consumer revolt against ground beef containing a particular added ingredient, known in the industry as lean finely textured beef (LFTB). LFTB includes trimmings of the cow that might otherwise go to waste, but that are processed in a way that allow them to be blended in with traditional ground beef. To the public, however, the additive came to be known by a new name: *pink slime*. Of course, that term induces an instant revulsion—it conveys a visceral sense that there is something wrong with the product.

The product and its unpleasant name seized the public imagination in a way that its benign competitor for mindshare ("Beef is beef") did not. What might explain the comparative power of the two frames? Part of the reason lies in the irresistibly vivid description. "Don't call it pink slime," moaned Georgia Agriculture Commissioner Gary Black. "Lean, finely textured beef is the proper name, and it is a safe, widely used product."[1] Do you think that worked? Of course not.

Pink slime only became an effective frame once it was picked up by the media—especially television. In fact, the term was coined in 2002 (shortly after it was approved for human consumption) by Gerald Zirnstein, a microbiologist for the USDA Food Safety and Inspection Service, in an internal e-mail. Two *New York Times* articles in 2009 and 2010 used the term. Yet that still did not provoke much of a response. It was only when *ABC News* presented a story in March 2012 that a major reaction occurred. Why? We would argue that it was because the frame was amplified by the method of communication. It is one thing to write "pink slime" in an e-mail or a newspaper column. It is quite another to emblazon the words on a television screen atop images of the least appetizing pseudo-meat you have ever seen. This created a visceral reaction—enough to trigger a widespread outcry and concerted action.

The *ABC News* exposé went viral, with grim consequences for the product's manufacturers. Three plants were closed by Beef Products Inc.; AFA Foods was forced to declare bankruptcy.[2] And, in another example of feeble framing, Cargill significantly cut production of the product and in April 2012 warned [that] "the public's resistance to the filler could lead to higher hamburger prices this barbecue season."[3]

Of course, frames often have unintended consequences. The pink slime nickname had a cost: closed factories, lost jobs, and many more cattle slaughtered to make up for the weight of what was now rejected.

Similarly, on political issues, frames are abundant. Advertising spending for the 2012 US presidential election reached almost $6 billion.[4] However, the framing war is not confined to these electoral leadership battles. "We are the 99 percent" was an evocative slogan that energized the Occupy Movement in 2011 and early 2012. The slogan refers to the fact that 99 percent of US households earn less than $506,000 per year, while the remaining 1 percent collectively take home a vastly disproportionate amount. A blog by a New York–based activist named Chris (not the author!) gave faces and voices to those falling through the cracks in American life through homelessness, welfare ineligibility, and other system failures. It is safe to say the total cost for that particular advertising campaign fell well short of $6 billion.

There are myriad other examples of framing in social issues. We can trace some frames back many years. For instance, "No taxation without representation" captured a primary grievance underpinning the American Revolution. It has stayed in popular consciousness as an important principle of government for 250 years! "Blood diamonds" became the frame of those working against the sale of diamonds to fund war efforts, especially in Africa. The movie *Blood Diamond,* starring Leonardo DiCaprio, raised this issue in the popular consciousness.

Framing within Organizations

Intrapreneurs need to navigate different cultures and competing strategic priorities within the same organization. Research by Sue Ashford from the University of Michigan suggests that the single most important tactic used by issue sellers is adapting their message to the audience they are approaching. Successful intrapreneurs use this knowledge to their advantage.[5]

Sometimes, differences within organizational culture are visible even from a distance. Imagine trying to get an initiative on accelerating women in business to take hold at Avon. The cosmetics company prides itself on building strong, personal relationships between its sales force of "Avon Ladies" and a primarily female customer base. Avon's tagline "The Company for Women" is self-explanatory, and it walks the talk by funding the Avon Foundation to undertake programs combating breast cancer and domestic violence. Yet, Avon is still clearly a for-profit corporation. Now try the same thing at Goldman Sachs, at the vanguard of capitalism, and where elements of its culture have been rendered more visible recently through the wonders of Twitter. The @GSElevator Twitter account reports allegedly overheard biased conversations to frame a misogynistic environment at the giant investment bank.[6] At which company do you think your pitch for accelerating women in business would find a more receptive culture?

While reading through the websites of the two companies, one would actually probably admire the programs that both support on this issue. Avon's program for women is front and center on its corporate home page. In fact, Goldman also has an inspiring program called 10,000 Women aimed at training female entrepreneurs in low-income countries. Why is this? The explanation may be found in the motivating factors for both companies.

Avon's products are marketed to women; its sales force is predominantly women. There is clear integrity between its business strategy and its philanthropic giving. The prime motivation appears to be in connecting better with its customer and employee base. Adopting a cause that is aligned is both the right thing to do and good business sense.

At Goldman, the situation is arguably quite different. Despite progress toward gender equality in recent years, insiders would admit that investment banking remains a business predominantly driven by men. Adopting economic advancement of women might seem like a good thing to do intrinsically, but it would be hard to connect it directly to the subjective happiness of the customer base or employees at Goldman Sachs. Instead, the motivation (beyond general brand benefits) for adopting programs for economic advancement for women lies in sustainable economic development. Research shows that the economic empowerment of women is a major contributing factor to the success of entire economies. Indeed, this was not a "soft" decision for Goldman. It only gave the green light to the 10,000 Women project after undertaking an exhaustive study on the economic impact of the issue via a major consulting firm. However, when it did decide to proceed, Goldman invested substantially in time and resources. The return on investment may be both in economic development (and eventually new markets for Goldman), and in attracting more women to the firm.[7]

By understanding that within a company there are competing cultures and leadership priorities, and a dynamic environment of issue selling, the skilled intrapreneur can learn to tailor messages to specific audiences.

Designing Effective Frames

Part of the reason that frames are so effective is that they can activate the *confirmation bias*—the idea that when we hold a hypothesis or explanation, we are prone to seeking and finding evidence in support of it and ignoring or discounting evidence that is inconsistent with it. The world is full of ambiguous or contradictory signals that can be read in different ways; the confirmation bias suggests that we tend to see evidence that fits the view we came in with. If you believe that a job applicant is unsuitable for a position, you are sure to find evidence consistent with that view, and vice versa. Observe that political debaters on the internet rarely lack for persuasive anecdotes that those in the other party are partisan, incompetent, uncooperative, greedy, and so on. Writer Jon Ronson once quipped that he had recently learned about the confirmation bias, and now he was seeing it everywhere.[8] Frames are like that.

An effective frame can diagnose problems, suggest solutions, or both. What's the problem? What can we do to address it? In chapter 4, we discussed how changes in the internal and external environment, including arising problems, open up new possibilities for creating change in organizations. Research by Sue Ashford and colleagues suggests that while it can be effective to point to good opportunities or solutions, what is especially important is that the opportunities or solutions presented align with the priorities of senior management. It is apparent from their interviews with 101 issue sellers in organizations that "the moral sell" is largely ineffective. In other words, attempting to convince leadership that something is "the right thing to do" rarely gets you very far.[9]

Does the paucity of evidence in support of the effectiveness of a moral sell mean that you should not even raise issues of right and wrong in organizations? Hardly. In *Tempered Radicals,* Debra Meyerson outlines the stories of many people who have bravely taken action against perceived injustices in the workplace with great success.[10] We were pleased to come across some of these remarkable individuals in our work too. However, it appears that the moral compass is rarely referenced in the final determination of a proposal's merits.

Thankfully, there are exceptions to this rule. Sometimes the right thing to do is accepted as a course of action even when it is not clearly the right thing for the bottom line of the business, at least in the short term. SC Johnson, a family-owned company that makes dozens of familiar household products such as Windex, Glade, and Ziploc bags, committed to removing chloride from all of its products. Chloride has harmful environmental and health side effects, and the company's leadership aimed to banish it from their production process. The company had been successful in doing this with all its products without harming the customer experience—until it came to Saran Wrap. The cling film has been a popular product for SC Johnson for decades, but efforts to reconfigure its chemistry to remove chloride disappointed several iterations of customer test groups. So company leadership was left with a difficult decision: keep the product unchanged and maintain customer satisfaction, or keep the commitment to remove chloride from all its products and risk losing the long-standing market leadership that SC Johnson had built around this product. They chose the latter and removed chloride despite the anticipated customer backlash. The result, as expected, has been a stark erosion of market share but a further demonstration of SC Johnson's commitment to doing what it feels is the right thing for its customers and the environment. As laudable as the decision may be, logic shows that companies can choose the moral side of these market-driven trade-offs only so often before economics forces their hand to stay in business.

Our advice is this: it can be effective to point out that a particular course of action is the right thing to do. However, we would not recommend making it the only element of the case you are making. Instead, seek to include it as part of a bundle of supporting arguments, and lead with the business case. Where the moral rationale can be integrated with supporting strong business outcomes, the likelihood of success in selling the initiative will increase.

Choosing a Frame That Fits

Frames that resonate within organizations typically reflect the corporate culture: the DNA of shared meanings, assumptions, and stories that shape how people understand the organization and its purpose. Frames need to be packaged and conveyed in a way that fits with the culture, but also in a way that speaks to diverse constituencies. As Elad Levinson, a senior organizational development professional and lifelong social intrapreneur, told us: "The test of a frame is that it should help everyone see the relevance to the company right away, while not causing anyone to be predisposed against the idea."

Chapter 4 described how culture can be thought of as the "theory of the business" that underlies strategies and structures in a system. Although every culture is unique, there are a few generic tendencies. High-tech Silicon Valley firms tend to look more like each other than they look like retailers or nonprofits. Managerial logics are one way to get at the rules of the game in a culture—what is valued and why. The dominant managerial logics are often made visible through the language used. In chapter 4, we described how to use content analysis to analyze corporate documents to diagnose the corporate culture. With this diagnosis in hand, it is possible to fit the case for your innovation to the organization's culture.

Table 5-1, from Northwestern University's Klaus Weber, provides a guide that can help you select appropriate elements for your frame. For each type of culture, it suggests what kinds of *benefits* to allude to (i.e., how does your innovation create value for the organization); what kind of *data* is considered persuasive in this organization; which kind of people are regarded

TABLE 5-1

Management logics and framing

Logic	Benefits	Authorities	Data	Delivery	Language
Inspired	Purpose, excitement, motivation, energy, direction, innovation	Visionaries, gurus, innovators, forward thinkers	Personal stories, images, metaphors, exemplars	Creative, storytelling, intuitive, emotional, unusual, enthusiastic	Challenge, adventure, dream, ambition, risk taking, path breaking, thrill, awe, faith, vision, passion
Family	Affirming values and traditions, loyalty, solidarity	Senior managers, experienced members	Precedents, traditions, founders' values and goals	Through hierarchical channels, respectful, affirmative	Harmony, tradition, solidarity, enduring, experience, leaders, virtue, wisdom, leaders, legacy, harmony
Popularity	Attention, awards, reputation, fame, recognition, brand	Opinion leaders, rising stars, media, celebrities	Rankings, buzz, momentum, stigma, opinion surveys	Attention-grabbing, spectacle, show number of supporters	Admiration, esteem, trend, publicity, making a splash, wow, visibility
Civic	Inclusion, engagement, common good	Cross-functional groups, committees	Mission statements, organizational policies, consensus, legal	Due process, debate, consensus, wide participation	Common interest, citizenship, cooperative, justice, principles, fairness, rights and duties
Market	Competitive advantage, revenue, market share	High performers, competitors, customers	Customer research, benchmarks, return on investment	Entrepreneurial, competitions (market for ideas), negotiation	Competition, demand, winning, price, wealth, fortune, economics, entrepreneurship, venture
Industrial	Efficiency, cost/ resource reduction, quality	Technical experts, professionals, certifiers and tools	Quantitative, plans, flowcharts, cost, budgets, measurement	Professional, analytic, thorough, evidence-based, objective	Efficient, analysis, plan, project, waste, optimization, resources, standardization
Sustainable	Future survival, balance interests	Stakeholders, abstract systems, (e.g., planet)	Ecological and social impacts, stakeholder voice, ethics	Authentic concern, stakeholder/community involvement	Balance, natural, ethical, ecosystem, pollution, footprint, impact, stewardship, healthy

Source: Klaus Weber, "Converging Orders of Worth: Adaptive and Demographic Mechanisms of Cultural Globalization," Kellogg School of Management Technical Note, forthcoming.

as *authorities*; how should you *deliver* your pitch; and what kind of *language* will be most compelling in this context.

How solutions are framed at the highest level should be adapted to the culture of the specific organization. Imagine you wanted to create a Corporate Service Corps in your company. Recall that the Corporate Service Corps is IBM's "corporate Peace Corps," and was initially received as a rather odd fit. Understanding the dominant logics would help adapt the frame with the greatest likelihood of success. For example, in IBM's "market"-dominated logic, winning the war for retaining the best talent against competitors was a frame that fit. In a company strong on the "civic" logic, like Cascade, arguing a strong business case with a flavor of developing responsible, ethical leaders may resonate. In a company like Whole Foods, with a strong "sustainable" logic, understanding the realities of its suppliers and supply chain in lower-income, developing markets may make a connection.

On a consulting project, Chris wanted to understand some of the dynamics between large breast-milk-substitute manufacturers on the one hand, and advocates for abolishing complementary feeding on the other. As many of you are probably aware, this is a heated, emotional issue, where both sides are highly entrenched in their positions. The advocacy groups will routinely call companies that produce breast-milk substitutes "babykillers," while the companies will point to reams of scientific studies that support the benefits of complementary feeding. Using a language analysis software tool, Chris was able to gain some insight into the culture of the companies and organizations involved and make recommendations for framing that might have the most chance of finding common ground. For instance, in examining publicly available documents from over twenty companies and advocacy groups involved in infant and young child nutrition, he discovered that while the "logics" used in some areas were very divergent, in others the gap between certain organizations was not as large as might be expected. In particular, one of the two main advocacy groups showed a strong bias toward the "market" management logic. This suggested that, although it would likely be very cautious in engaging, it might be more open to dialogue based on business-oriented solutions to global health issues than the other main advocacy group. This agreement on some cultural values suggested a potential starting point for engagement.

Reference points vary within organizations. What counts as an authority in a given culture? Who gets listened to, and who does not? In our conversations with intrapreneurs, we were surprised by how often business press such as *McKinsey Quarterly* or *The Economist* were cited as being a source of credible resources to inform decision making. Gib Bulloch told us that "One article in the *Financial Times* is worth twenty internal e-mails" in terms of its persuasive power. While these are sources of insightful commentary, they do not always provide the raw data upon which analytical decisions can be made. Instead, they influence what even gets to the discussion table in the first place. This is further proof that framing influences how the data itself gets considered.

Crafting a Narrative

Think of a frame as a *narrative,* which may literally be a story but need not be. A good narrative can take the form of stories, imagery, numbers, or exemplars (SINE). Often, the best narratives employ all four at different times to maximize impact.

Stories

Storytelling repeatedly emerged in our interviews as a key skill of successful intrapreneurs. Indeed, the excellent Aspen Institute's First Movers Fellowship Program for social intrapreneurs spends a considerable amount of time helping participants to hone the way they narrate themselves and the initiatives they are spearheading.

As an internet marketing manager at eBay, Robert Chatwani applied his personal experiences from visiting family in India to develop and internally sell the business model for a fair-trade marketplace. The vividness and emotion of his personal connection to his vision helped the idea come alive. Through conversation with artisans in India, he had kept hearing the same refrain: *"We need more shoppers like you; greater access to markets. We would be able to create so much more opportunity for ourselves, our families, our communities, if we just had more people buying our goods."* Upon his return to the United States, Chatwani, an up-and-coming leader at eBay, shared his idea to link the goods of talented artisans with new markets in the West. He found an encouraging audience in founder Pierre Omidyar, then-CEO Meg Whitman, and other key players. The door was open to social innovation.

Chatwani's personal experience in India offered credibility and generated new conversations. However, he also went through a painstaking process of internal selling over a prolonged period of time. It was clear that there was a potentially viable business that built on eBay's competencies in hosting online platforms to connect buyers and sellers, although it was likely to appeal to a somewhat different demographic from eBay's core. It was also clear that local producers in low-income countries could reach a much broader audience of consumers if they had access to eBay's platform. During this time, Chris would regularly go to meet with Chatwani at eBay and be shown the updated beta version of the website, the latest research on target consumers ("our target market are the LOHAS—lifestyles of health and sustainability—consumers; we need to learn everything we can about them"), and yet another set of PowerPoint slides tweaked for the exact internal audience of the day. The story was strong, and it was adapted to each particular stakeholder.

The idea, and the story, had a successful launch. The marketplace was eventually called World of Good—eBay bought the rights to the name of its core partner in the Fair Trade venture, feeling its brand could best help achieve their shared goals.[11]

Imagery

A picture may be worth more than a thousand words to social innovators. A single image can create an emotional reaction that only the worlds greatest orators can emulate. Indeed, so powerful are images that before I have given a single example, some images are probably already coming into your mind. Consider the example of Thich Quang Duc. "Who?" you might ask. But you'll probably recognize his picture (figure 5-1).

Many of you will have seen this harrowing photograph, captured by Associated Press journalist Malcolm Browne. Tape recordings captured the reaction of President John F. Kennedy to first seeing the photo. Kennedy was on a telephone call with Attorney General Robert Kennedy when he was shown the pictures. "Jesus Christ!" he gasped. Kennedy later remarked, "No news picture in history has generated so much emotion

FIGURE 5-1

Source: Copyright © 1963 AP Photo/Malcolm Browne

around the world as that one." Five months and five more tragic self-immolations later, Vietnamese president Ngô Đình Diệm was overthrown in a coup and assassinated the next day.

While such tragedies and their jarring images are unnecessary to influence inside organizations, our interviewees often recounted stories of powerful pictures catalyzing a mood change in decision makers. Sometimes, intrapreneurs are able to use visual images to appeal to leaders' sense of hope and possibility. One change agent in a large consulting firm described how he had mocked up a convincing—but fake—*Time* magazine cover showcasing the program that he was building. He left it on the desk of a senior leader he was trying to influence—and received a supportive, and good-humored, call soon after.

In organizations, data visualization is often used to communicate effectively. Consultants and teachers know the power of the "killer slide," the one that often condenses months of rigorous data analysis into a single chart. The chart is normally simple, elegantly communicating the core insight of the project in a way that hundreds of words could not. While on a project with a large pharmaceutical company, Chris was repeatedly shown one slide from a deck produced by a major consulting firm three years previously that had helped make the case for launching a new business unit. In the folklore of how the business unit had developed, it was clear that this slide deck had been incredibly influential over an extended period of time. It ranked the potential within certain geographies based on population size and per capita income. The prized slide was a chart that showed a range of seemingly ripe opportunities. Interestingly though, upon further analysis, the data was not as clear-cut as it seemed. One small adjustment to the way the data was presented had altered the logical conclusion viewers drew from "only one country in this region has a potentially viable market for our products" to "here are a range of potentially viable markets for our products." The use of a small line break on one axis materially impacted the terms of discussion around prioritization of markets for consideration. While the ethics of using such framing tricks to adjust how data is interpreted must be carefully considered, it is undeniable that visual frames strongly influence the outcome of the discussion.

Marcos Mancini, an alumnus of our MBA class on social intrapreneurship, was able to depict networks and market systems in a way that helped the company understand the opportunity at hand. Marcos helped the Latin American bank Banorte bridge into microfinance. His first project was to map the impact investing ecosystem in Latin American so that the team could make informed decisions about where to best participate, if at all. The sophistication of the data visualization helped draw people into Marcos's narrative.

Numbers

Being able to quantify a grievance or an opportunity is especially important in organizations. When we asked IBM's Kevin Thompson, "What do you wish you had learned in business school to help you as an intrapreneur?" he paused. His response: "I think you should make students take three finance classes as prerequisites before letting them take the class. If they can't do the numbers, then they won't have any credibility in our kind of company." As an intrapreneur, Kevin had to deal with the perception of his personal brand as being a former Peace Corps guy. Being especially strong at the quantitative end of the business helped him limit any assumptions based on this stereotype that he was not suited to the core business. It must have paid off for him: he is now in the executive ranks at Big Blue. Similarly, when we spoke with Justin DeKoszmovszky when he was at SC Johnson, he acknowledged that many tactics work for getting the issue on the table—but at the end of the day, the decision would be made largely based on the numbers. This is a message that has been reinforced across most of our conversations with intrapreneurs.

What do we mean by *numbers*? For intrapreneurs in most organizations, it is largely "consultant math"—working with spreadsheets to understand the economics of the proposal on the table, and then being able to distill the complexity down to the bare essentials that matter most to your particular audiences. Figuring out how best to communicate the quantitative messages is part of the intrapreneur's art.

Examples that are able to combine imagery and numbers often have an even greater impact. Think of the tobacco industry. Imagery has been powerful in encouraging people to smoke (consider the Marlboro Man riding free on the prairie). It has also been powerful in discouraging people from smoking (think of the images you have seen of blackened lungs in health warnings).

In organizations, quantifying impact is especially effective—and often essential. In a business context, Puma communicated an innovation to reduce packaging waste through its Clever Little Bag. The materials issued in support of the release were littered with numbers: reducing cardboard usage by 65 percent; saving 8,500 tons of paper, 20 million megajoules of electricity, 1 million liters of water, 1 million liters of fuel oil, and 500,000 liters of diesel; reducing carbon dioxide by 10,000 tons.[12] All of these improvements to Puma's environmental footprint inevitably saved money too: a win for both environmentally conscious consumers and to the corporate bottom line. The videos on YouTube communicating the initiative have had more than 400,000 viewers—free mindshare gained by the company.

Exemplars

An exemplar personalizes the issue—creating role models or simply giving it a human face. Personalizing the issue at hand helps people understand it and connect to it on an emotional level. In social and political movements, politicians understand this well. "Joe the Plumber" shot to national fame in the 2008 election after asking candidate Obama about how his taxes as a small businessman might go up if Obama were president. Although Joe the Plumber was an actual person—Samuel Joseph Wurzelbacher—he also served as an archetype representing ordinary working

Americans who might want to own their own business one day. The debate over which candidate would best serve Joe's needs and interests played a prominent role in the campaign.

Such personalization often increases efficacy in attracting people to support your cause. Research by Katherine Burson at the University of Michigan shows that people give more money to charity when they are presented with an individual or with a cohesive collective rather than a statistic or with a large number of otherwise unrelated people.[13]

In organizations, this is also a common practice. Rather than just give abstract descriptions of target markets, marketing professionals try to bring this down to an individual level. They even give names such as "Helen Housewife" or "Tom Teacher" to depict gender, age-group, and occupation in a way that dry data cannot.

For social intrapreneurs, too, the practice of personalizing the issue—of providing exemplars—increases the likelihood of success. In early 2012, there was a spate of high-profile laboratory accidents in academic settings. Controls for safety in labs are much more stringent in industry than in academia. This led several people at Dow Chemical to consider how they might best contribute to safer conditions. When making the case to senior leadership for creating the Dow Lab Safety Academy, rather than speaking in generalizations or making a crass business case, an up-and-coming Dow executive drew on the story of the recent tragic death of an undergraduate student in a laboratory fire to support his argument of urgency.[14] For leaders in the room with daughters of a similar age to the young woman who lost her life in the fire, the message really struck home. Thus, Dow's new initiative was able to strengthen the company's ties with universities and reinforce its reputation for having a strong safety culture, while making a measurable and important reduction on the number of lab fires on college campuses each year.[15]

Putting It All Together

By using stories, images, numbers, and exemplars effectively, intrapreneurs can increase the likelihood that their messages will be retained—and even go viral. When used together, these elements can be especially effective. We will take an example first in social movements, and then in social innovation organizational change efforts.

The Arab Spring

Let us begin with the horrific events that served as a catalyst for the Arab Spring. Khaled Said was a young Egyptian man who was beaten to death by two police officers in June 2010. While police brutality is appalling and offensive to our sense of justice, it is sadly not uncommon in many countries. But the consequences in this case took on a scale much larger than could otherwise have been expected. Why might this have been?

> **Stories:** The frame that was chosen was powerful. "We are all Khaled Said," a Facebook page launched by a Google marketing executive as a show of solidarity, became a unifying cry. "We are all Khaled Said" was meant to induce outrage, fellow feeling, and the sense of being part of a movement bigger than oneself. It succeeded.

> **Imagery:** The visual imagery was critical. Said had been publicly beaten to death by police officers. His head was smashed into iron doors on the way to the police car, and he was

repeatedly hit even after he appeared to have lost consciousness or died. Said suffered a dislocated jaw, broken nose, fractured skull, and other injuries. His brother took photographs of Said in the morgue, which were set beside recent photos of the young, handsome man he had been before the assault. The contrast was shocking, and the images went viral in a way that words never could. The *Washington Post* said, "Had it not been for a leaked morgue photo of his mangled corpse, tenacious relatives and the power of Facebook, the death of Khaled Said would have become a footnote in the annals of Egyptian police brutality. Instead, outrage over the beating death of the 28-year-old man in [Alexandria] last summer, and attempts by local authorities to cover it up, helped spark the mass protests demanding the ouster of Egyptian President Hosni Mubarak."[16]

Numbers: The Facebook page offered a way for people around the world to visibly show their support for the family and friends of Khaled Said. This they did, in droves. By the end of January 2011, the page had more than 470,000 followers.[17] As well as putting pressure on the Egyptian government to act, the support shown was likely a factor in encouraging those in other countries to take action. This perceived safety in numbers created conditions conducive to a domino effect of uprisings.

Exemplars: The outcry over Khaled Said's death was much greater than might have been expected because of the intense personification of the issue. Said might have been our friend, our brother, our son. We could relate to him in a way that would be impossible had he remained anonymous: nameless, with no before-and-after photos.

The brutal killing of Khaled Said mobilized public outrage against the Egyptian government. This reaction was fueled by the stories, imagery, numbers, and exemplar that were brought together to drive the message

Cascade Engineering

Now let's turn our attention to Cascade Engineering, whose Welfare-to-Career program bears testament to the principle that persistence pays off.

Stories: As Cascade has rolled out its Welfare-to-Career program, leaders have been able to tell the stories of individuals whose lives have been impacted. Hundreds of people have moved out of welfare programs and been able to build careers at Cascade, with profoundly positive outcomes for themselves, the company, and their families.

Imagery: Painting the picture of the extended impact of transitioning from welfare to career helped make the case for the multiple efforts to launch the program success-fully at Cascade. Becoming self-sufficient economically and professionally has helped build the self-esteem of the program participants. It provides positive role models to family members and children. It reduces crime. All of these outcomes—beyond the direct money saved by the company and the State of Michigan—help tell a richer story.

Numbers: The program reduced turnover costs for the company by over $3 million in nine years. Numbers like this help build the case during the cycle of internal sell-ing, as projections and forecasts. As the program is up and

FIGURE 5-2

Source: Photo use by arrangement with Cascade Engineering

running, these numbers can help build the case for continued investment and scaling of initiatives.

Exemplars: Here is Amy (figure 5-2). Look her in the eyes. Personalizing makes a difference. Amy is not an abstract idea. She is not a number. She is not a program. She is someone who gained a career fourteen years ago through the Welfare-to-Career program at Cascade. There are not just five hundred people who have participated in this program. There are five hundred people like Amy.

Taking a Frame to Market

Taking a frame to market is a process of iteration and refinement. The first attempt at framing is unlikely to be the final story. As you begin discussing your initiative with people, you can listen carefully to their reactions to make adjustments as you go. Through this process of iteration, you will eventually settle on a master frame that works well for your purposes. You can look for occasions when people are adopting your frame as the basis for their own arguments—this is an indicator that it is being adopted as one of the dominant managerial logics in your organization.

Even with the right frame, the success of your initiative will also depend on who you introduce your frame to first. This leads us to chapter 6, where we will consider the importance of understanding the networks in which you operate.

CHAPTER SIX

Who: Understanding Social Networks

Shortly after accounting giants Price Waterhouse and Coopers & Lybrand merged in 1998, a pair of young interns based in London—Amy Middleberg from the United States and New Zealander James Shaw—were asked their thoughts on what kind of values should guide the newly christened PricewaterhouseCoopers (PwC).[1] They took the challenge seriously and proposed a bold idea—for PwC to become in essence a triple-bottom-line business that measured not just financial performance, but social and environmental performance as well. Moreover, they believed that PwC could begin by creating a social audit that drew on the accounting firm's core competencies and that could serve clients aiming to track their own social performance. With the audacity of youth, they recruited an ally, Fabio Sgaragli, who had joined the firm to work on merger integration (which, not incidentally, provided insights into potential allies and non-allies in the new firm). They also boldly managed to convince Jermyn Brooks, a global managing partner, of the merits of their idea. This in turn led to meetings with other important influencers in the new company; each received a customized pitch, highlighting brand differentiation (for those focused on marketing), implementation (for those focused on strategic change), and so on. The three used a low-tech version of network analysis and customer relationship management, using flip charts to map out the positions of members of the global leadership team, how supportive they were, and how they were connected to the group's converts. They rapidly managed to be named as team leads for the project.

These ambitious and talented interns were a textbook example of innovation as a social movement. They found the right opportunity in the merger of Price Waterhouse and Coopers & Lybrand, which opened the new firm to significant changes in values and strategy. They framed their proposal in a way that fit with the core strategy and competence of the firm, while customizing their pitch to the priorities of the audience. And they analyzed the networks of potential allies and their links to decision makers, using the resources available to them. Despite being relatively inexperienced and unconnected to influencers in the new organization, Middleberg, Shaw, and Sgaragli were able to get approval to take their proposal forward.

In chapters 4 and 5, we showed how information technology tools can help with the first two tasks—analyzing the culture and customizing the frame. In this chapter, we delve into social network analysis, which provides tools for analyzing and visualizing social networks. The informal flip-chart analysis can be made more precise and more effective with a few tools that were not yet readily available when Middleberg and Shaw made their pitch.

Networks and How They Matter

Social networks are a way of describing relationships between people and organizations. Online tools like Facebook highlight friendship networks, but networks can consist of any kind of tie—collaboration, advice, resource exchange, even "enemy" networks. Scholars have mapped networks of who dates whom in an Ohio high school; which physicists collaborate together; what characters appear together in scenes from, say, *Les Misérables*; which species feed on each other in an ecosystem; and who gave tuberculosis to whom in an epidemic. Google's original PageRank algorithm, which ranked websites according to their likely relevance, did this by analyzing the networks created by web pages pointing to other web pages via links.[2]

More recently, it has come to light that the NSA uses telephone metadata—records of who called whom, and for how long—to map the social networks of essentially every telephone customer in the United States and beyond. Although the putative aim of the effort was to identify terrorist networks, the resulting data set was surely a marketer's dream.[3]

Networks can be mapped and measured, providing graphic and quantitative ways of assessing the social landscape. Network measures like *centrality* provide an objective way of rating importance. Google shows the value of being able to quantify network centrality for websites. More recently, Klout and other start-ups have begun to provide online influence scores drawing on social network analysis techniques.

In this chapter, we describe methods for gathering network data and using it to map the social structure of an organization, including locating the most critical people who can help (or hinder) your innovation. Research shows that networks often have properties that are useful for thinking about the spread of innovations. For instance, neurons in worm brains, Hollywood movie stars who appear in the same films together, and networks of corporate directors all have the property of being a *small world*—that is, the average shortest distance between pairs of people, or neurons, is surprisingly short.[4] This generally happens because there are a handful of especially well-connected people or organizations who shorten the paths for the rest of us. We all know that one person who seems to know everybody and who can often get us the introduction we need. In the corporate world in 2001, a flu virus that infected the JP Morgan Chase board in January would have spread to roughly 80 percent of the *Fortune* 1000 by May via monthly board meetings. Being able to locate the right kinds of supporters can make all the difference in spreading contagious innovations too.[5]

Understanding networks can help with several key parts of leading a movement:

Recruiting: Having friends active in a movement is often more important for converting people into activists than the strength of their convictions. Network ties can be used to help reach out and recruit new supporters.[6]

Information: A well-structured network of support that spans different parts of the organization can provide an early warning system about changes and opportunities that might affect your innovation.[7]

Legitimation: Having the visible support of the right allies, and avoiding the wrong opponents, is crucial to getting a social innovation to take flight. These supporters can be like the board of directors of an IPO firm, giving comfort to potential "investors" that the innovation is a good bet.

Contagion: Understanding the structure of a network makes it possible to target energies most effectively on those mostly likely to help an initiative spread quickly. To continue the analogy used above, sneezing at a JP Morgan Chase board meeting would have a much greater potential effect than sneezing at the board meeting of a small start-up.

How to Get Network Data

The examples earlier in the chapter hinted that network data is all around us, if we know what to look for. Who calls whom, who has worked together on projects, who eats lunch together, who is connected on LinkedIn or Facebook, who volunteers at the same nonprofit—all of these are more-or-less visible traces of different types of relationships. Getting network data entails turning these traces of everyday life into something solid for analysis. If you can turn them into entries in a spreadsheet, you can analyze a network.

Several years ago, Chris was engaged on a consulting project to help foster constructive discussion on a controversial global health issue. To begin to identify who he might bring together in dialogue, he gathered all the attendee lists for meetings and conferences on this topic for the last five years. He looked for occasions when attendees had been at similar events as a way to begin to identify individuals with common interests. By doing so, he was able to find a group of individuals with whom a constructive conversation could begin due to their common set of references.

The goal of network analysis is to understand the broader terrain that all these relationships together create. Perhaps the most pervasive repository of network data is the company's e-mail server. For many employees, e-mail is a nearly universal means of communication within the organization, even for coworkers in the office next door. E-mail provides an easy medium to keep track of commitments and assemble a to-do list, and provides virtual paper trail to document progress. Many of us use the e-mail system as a filing system and to-do list.

To a network analyst, it is also a gold mine. Having just the "To" and "From" lines and the date—without the actual content of the messages—can provide the raw materials for detailed social mapping. Of course, this feature has not gone unnoticed by those in the business of regulation and law enforcement. During its investigation of the Enron collapse, the Federal Energy Regulatory Commission (FERC) acquired hundreds of thousands of e-mails between 150 of Enron's senior managers, which have subsequently been made available to researchers and the general public.[8] (You can download them yourself if you have a spare half-gigabyte of storage space.)

Naturally, corporations have become quite attentive to what their employee e-mails reveal. There are now dozens of software applications that allow companies to mine employee e-mail data to flag suspicious activity. What counts as "suspicious"? This might include e-mailing groups with whom one does not have an obvious connection (which, in some cases, such as financial institutions, is a red flag for fraud) or sending inconsistent messages. A word to the wise: whatever you send by e-mail is likely to be archived and analyzed by your IT staff. Moreover, some of the activities of social intrapreneurs could look, from some angles, like "suspicious activity." We take this topic up in more detail in chapter 7.

You don't have to become one of the less sympathetic characters in an Orwell novel to gather useful data. There are other ways to gather network data that yields perhaps less intrusive information. *Affiliation data* comes from ties that people share by being in the same group. For instance, students who are officers of the same club, people who served on a task force together, coworkers who worked on the same engagement team, or MBAs who graduated in the same class share an affiliation. Of course, not all members of a twenty-person task force are necessarily on intimate terms. The thousand or so members of a given graduating class from Harvard Business School may recognize each other on sight, but the odds are good that they were not roommates or even classmates. Deciding whether a relationship between any two people is likely to exist can be more a matter of art than science. Even complete metadata on the phone calls of all customers of AT&T and Verizon may reveal a lot of "relationships" with the cable company's 800 number, and few relationships at all among teenagers (who might instead use Snapchat to communicate with each other).

All that being said, there are a large number of potential unobtrusive sources of network information available to the inventive investigator. We thank the MBA students from our class on social intrapreneurship for sharing their own (seemingly NSA-inspired!) ideas here:

- **Data available at work:** The organization chart for reporting relationships; the employee directory for membership in the same department; staffing rosters for engagement teams, client teams, and task forces; who has worked with the same clients; shared membership on e-mail groups; e-mail networks based on who is cc'ed on messages; Outlook calendars for who has attended the same meetings; badge entry data from security systems that indicates who has been in meetings together; office sports teams; membership in affinity groups; who sits together at lunch; carpools; who opts in to bus passes; who lives in common neighborhoods.

- **Sources available online:** Twitter followers; LinkedIn contacts; LinkedIn groups; partner profiles on Facebook; who's tagged in the same pictures on Facebook; blogs and who responds; blogrolls and other links in/out; common topics at TED or on LinkedIn; member composition of Wikis and other forums for collaboration; WikiScanner data for editors and collaborators; coauthors and copanelists at conferences; GuideStar.org for nonprofit board memberships.

- **Slightly shadier sources:** Residing at the same address; membership in the same homeowners association; school alumni databases; membership on private-school boards of trustees; community newspaper reports; cosponsorship of charity events or board memberships; who's active in local places of worship; sinister person-tracing websites such as anywho.com.

A Brief and Nerdy Digression on Network Data

Before going into more detail on network data, it is useful to clarify some things about social network analysis because some of the measures we describe might be confusing otherwise. For most of its life as an area of study, social network analysis relied heavily on questionnaires to get at networks. People might be given lists of names of their coworkers and asked, "How often do you work with this person on common tasks or projects? How often do you see them socially (e.g., going out for lunch)? Who would you go to for advice on an important work-related matter?" This information describes the *ego network* around a particular individual.

If everyone at a workplace filled out the same questionnaire, we would have information on the *global network* at that workplace. We would expect to see that, for questions like "How often do you work with this person?" or "How often do you see this person socially?" both people would give roughly the same answer. Such data is undirected or *symmetric*. (In practice, we often find that people give divergent answers; I might say that we work together daily, and you might say you have never seen me before.) For other questions, we do not expect the answers to be symmetric. The fact that I go to you for advice on important work-related matters does not imply that you would reciprocate—after all, you are the expert, not me. The data in this case is directed.

Some kinds of data are inherently symmetric or undirected. Affiliation data in general is undirected. All of us who serve together on the board of a nonprofit organization or who were assigned to the same client engagement team are symmetrically connected. Facebook friendships are also undirected (although, of course, knowing who friended whom would make a friend relationship directed). On the other hand, data such as telephone or e-mail "metadata"—information about who called or e-mailed whom—is directed because one party initiates the "tie." (Being listed together on the cc: line in an e-mail, however, is undirected.)

The distinction between directed and undirected ties is important because some measures only make sense for one kind of data. Symmetric data on advice networks is not very useful: the person on the receiving end of a lot of requests for advice is an expert, while the person on the sending end is probably not.

Many of the measures we care about require directed data. We need to know which direction the information flows. Treating all ties as undirected could lead you astray—you might confuse a maven with a connector (don't worry, this will make sense shortly).

Finding the Right People for Your Movement Using Network Analysis

What, exactly, do we want to know about a network? This can be organized into a few key questions, which generally correspond to specific network measures.

Who Is Important?

Put more precisely, this question asks who is *central* in the network? Network scholars have proposed dozens of centrality measures because there are many different ways to be "important" in a network. We focus on four of them that are particularly useful for leading innovations[9]:

- The simplest is *degree*: how many people am I connected to? Degree can be directed or undirected. Ties coming in (for instance, how many people come to you for advice) are called *in-degree*, while ties going out (how many people you ask for advice) are *out-degree*. The number of people you serve on boards with is an undirected measure of degree.

- A second and somewhat intuitive measure is *closeness*: how easily can I reach everybody else? Think of this as a "friends-of-friends" or "degrees of separation" measure. On average, how many friends would I need to get an introduction to the average other person?

- A third measure is *betweenness*: how often am I on the shortest path between other people? This measure highlights the flow of information through a network. Frequent air travelers in North America might think of this as the Atlanta airport measure. What airport have you been stuck in most frequently en route to other places? For many of us, it is Atlanta, because our travels so often take us through this hub.

- Finally, the *eigenvector* measure: how well connected are those to whom I am connected? Am I popular with the popular kids, who have lots of other friends, or the other nerds, who have few? The eigenvector measure is closely related to the original Google search algorithm. Earlier search engines might gauge a website's importance by how many other websites point to it—that is, its degree; Google's method weighted these ties by how important they are.

How Dense or Well Connected Is the Network?

Is this a small town, where everybody knows each other, or is it Manhattan, where we are mutually anonymous? The density (or sparseness) of the network—the extent to which people all know each other—is important because it is easier to spread a virus when everyone is well connected, as parents of pre-schoolers in daycare can attest. On the other hand, opposition to innovation can be fierce in a place that is *too* well connected. Consider a branch office of a newly acquired bank in which everyone is highly comfortable using the familiar customer relationship management system, and they are now being asked to switch to the new corporate standard. An office that is well connected internally but disconnected externally is likely to pose more of a challenge to change than groups that are more dispersed.

Are There Groups or Cliques in the Organization?

Cliques or groups often take the form of departmental silos. Do people from the same department or office always eat lunch together, or do they branch out? In one of Jerry's studies of office design and innovation networks, he examined an organization that had an explicit policy of mixing up offices to generate cross-functional collaborations and innovation. The study included fancy regression equations to see how physical distance influenced the propensity of any two professionals to collaborate. But one look at a map color-coded by departmental affiliation made it immediately clear that everything was swamped by functional departments: the vast majority of professionals *never* collaborated with those in other functions, although they often collaborated with functional colleagues, regardless of where their office was.[10]

Cliques also form after a merger, when employees of the merging organizations continue to hang out with their former coworkers even after the merger takes place. Social network analysis provides a useful tool for measuring post-merger integration.[11]

Why Does the Network Look Like This?

This question is more interpretive than quantitative, but the shape of a company's network can give important clues about how things get done. For instance, are there particular choke points—people who are at the center of everything—in the network? Why or why not?

Different measures pose different demands for information. Of course, we rarely have access to the kind of detailed network information that, say, the NSA or a corporate IT department does, but it is still worth understanding what kinds of data are useful. Degree is the simplest measure of centrality and does not even require software—it is simply a count. Look up people's profiles on Facebook and you can quickly see how many "friends" they have—that is, their "degree centrality in the friendship network." LinkedIn has an app that allows you to quickly visualize your ties to your immediate network, or your ego network. You can easily break this down into in-degree and out-degree: how many people in your immediate network come to you for advice or guidance? How many people do you reach out to for advice?

But many of the more interesting measures require relatively complete information on the relevant network. A term that is useful here is *geodesic*, which is the shortest path between a pair of people (nodes). Think of it this way: imagine you had to fly Southwest Airlines from Savannah, Georgia, to Coeur d'Alene, Idaho. Unlike many airlines, which use a hub-and-spoke system, Southwest flies only point-to-point routes. What is the smallest number of segments you could book to get there? That is the geodesic.

The closeness measure asks, "What is the average shortest distance (geodesic length) between me and everybody else?" The shorter the path between you and everyone else, the easier it is to gather or spread information. The betweenness measure of centrality asks, "How often am I on the shortest path between all other pairs of people in the network?" To the extent that all paths lead through you, you are more central in betweenness. To continue the metaphor, you are like the Atlanta airport.

The eigenvector measure requires a surprising amount of computing power to calculate, because it simultaneously asks how central are you and all of your contacts, and all of their contacts, and so on. It tells us the relative *power* of our network.

Sometimes we have the luxury of doing network surveys, asking people questions like "Who would you go to if you needed advice on a business matter?" or "How often have you socialized with . . . ?" In the absence of this much data, it is still useful to consider approximations of these measures.

Linking the Metrics to the Concepts

In *The Tipping Point,* his popular account of how ideas and trends gain prominence, Malcolm Gladwell states, "When we are trying to make an idea or attitude or product tip, we're trying to change our audience in some small yet critical respect: we're trying to infect them, sweep them up in our epidemic, convert them from hostility to acceptance. That can be done through the influence of special kinds of people…" Those people are mavens, connectors, and salesmen. Although perhaps a bit imprecise, these are useful ideas for thinking about network measures:[12]

- *Mavens* are people whom others seek out for advice or information. Mavens are seen as a credible source of information, and thus they are especially useful to have on your side as an innovator. If you were in a position to mount a network survey, in-degree in the advice network would be an excellent measure of being a maven. In lieu of a survey, mavens are often distinguished by their nerdiness and their exceptionally detailed answers to questions. Mavens can also be located more informally by asking a few informants "Who should I go to in order to find out about . . . ?" When many people nominate the same person, that's a good indication that he or she is a maven.

- *Connectors* are those who are especially well networked in the organization. Although they may not always have a formal position of authority, they are often respected for being in the know. In network terms, being a connector is indicated by being high in eigenvector or betweenness centrality (these are different measures but often highly correlated). Some signs of being a connector include being included on many task forces, being recognized across many departments, and having a career path that spans many areas. If you ask, "Who should I talk to in order to get a better understanding of how things work around here?" you are likely to turn up the names of connectors.

- *Salespeople* are those who are particularly persuasive, although their positions, of course, need not be in sales or marketing. These individuals have a particular gift for getting others to nod in agreement. Salespeople are especially effective when they have a low closeness score (that is, they are few steps from everyone else), as this means their message has less distance to travel. Less formally, effective salespeople might be recognized by the extent to which their comments are retweeted or quoted.

Planning for Going Viral

Suppose you wanted to spread a happy virus in your company—a virus that is conveyed through face-to-face contact and that instills three months' worth of quiet calm and optimism in those who get it, with no untoward side effects. It turns out that the coming quarter is one of the most critical ever for the company. Who would you infect first?

If you were a typical reader, your answer might be, "The CEO, because she meets six times per year with the board and even more often with the top team." This would be the trickle-down theory of epidemiology. A network analyst such as yourself, on the other hand, would state with some confidence, "The people with the highest eigenvector centrality in the 'task' network, and those with the lowest 'closeness' centrality." Naturally, you would be correct. If you want something to go viral, it helps to find the right vector, as the epidemiologists say, and that is rarely the CEO.

Consider Typhoid Mary, one of the most infamous disease vectors in history. Mary Mallon was an asymptomatic sufferer of typhoid fever who worked as a cook in several restaurants and households in New York in the early twentieth century. Everywhere she worked, the people who ate her food came down with typhoid fever. Mary herself eschewed standard practices of kitchen hygiene, such as washing her hands, and was convinced that she was not sick—after all, she had no symptoms. By moving from kitchen to kitchen, she was an especially effective agent of infection. Indeed, it is hard to think of an occupation with a greater potential for starting an epidemic. It's not difficult to think of positions in many organizations that offer the same infectious capacity.

The term *going viral* is both imprecise and unappetizing as a metaphor for championing an innovation. Unlike typhoid fever (or Grumpy Cat and *Gangnam Style*), support for an innovation does not spread through sneezes or forwarded e-mails, but takes active recruitment. (The *Kony 2012* campaign, in which a You-Tube video decrying a Ugandan warlord was viewed millions of times and prompted a renewed effort toward his capture, provides a rare counter-example). Doug McAdam at Stanford studied the place of networks in recruitment of college students for Freedom Summer, and what he found was surprising. Before the passage of the Voting Rights Act in 1965, African Americans in the Deep South faced systematic barriers to voting, including poll taxes, lengthy tests, and in some cases campaigns of violent intimidation. Freedom Summer in 1964 was an effort to register as many African American voters as possible in Mississippi, where registration rates were vastly lower in 1964 than they had been in 1890. Registration endangered both prospective voters and those doing the registering. The Freedom Summer workers—black Mississippians as well as white college students from the North—suffered arrests, beatings, intimidation, and in several cases, death for this cause.

Although many students had expressed an interest in being part of Freedom Summer when recruitment happened on their campus, only a subset eventually made their way to Mississippi. What distinguished those who went from those who stayed home? Greater commitment? Higher moral standards? More physical strength? Surprisingly, the most critical distinguishing feature was networks—that is, how many friends were going.[13]

An immediate implication of this and other work on network contagion is that having well-connected allies, and particularly those who can convey their support to others persuasively, can be critical to getting your innovation to go viral. Connectors are particularly useful here. Connectors generally have a lot of friends. More importantly, they have friends who themselves have a lot of friends. When connectors get a virus, it's a safe bet that eventually many others will too.

It is not just being well connected that matters, however. It is also important that some allies have credibility within the organization. Mavens make especially useful champions. Having mavens in your corner can go far toward getting acceptance for your innovation and overcoming skepticism. The young PwC interns mentioned at the beginning of this chapter were especially savvy about locating appropriate potential allies for their proposed "social audit" practice and customizing their pitch to each one. They did not have fancy network mapping software to use, but their method was nonetheless effective.

Network mapping can also help figure out who is on the shortest path to those you want to recruit, once you know who they are. Jerry was hoping to find an opportunity to meet George W. Bush in order to share some thoughts on Bush's presidency. But the former president and Jerry tend to travel in different circles. Nonetheless, thanks to the "small world" property of social networks, Jerry was certain that Bush could not be that distant. As it happens, a colleague and collaborator at the University of Michigan, Marina Whitman, was a prominent economist who had served on a large number of major corporate boards, including JP Morgan Chase, Alcoa, Westinghouse, Unocal, Procter & Gamble, and others. Conveniently, Bush's vice president, Dick Cheney, had served on the Procter & Gamble board with Whitman during the 1990s. That meant that Jerry was only three degrees of separation from Bush. Whitman had also served on the Alcoa board with Paul O'Neill, the company's CEO and Bush's treasury secretary, and knew several other cabinet members through government and corporate service. All it would take was a couple of phone calls. It's a small world after all, as the song says.

Not everyone can be recruited just by a good pitch. Thoughtful networkers draw on existing connections from the core group to their peers. One of our intrapreneurs notes a particular type that makes for an appealing recruit: someone who has been with the organization for a few years, has social concerns, and is feeling restless, potentially contemplating a move. Involving such people with a social innovation can serve multiple interests at once: the recruit is able to pursue a valued purpose, the initiative gains talent, and the company is able to hang on to someone they might otherwise have lost.

In summary, after recruiting an initial brain trust of allies for your innovation and developing your frame in a way that fits with the organization's culture and priorities, it is useful to target connectors and mavens as potential ambassadors for your innovation. They can be located formally through network analysis, or informally through asking around in a directed way.

Building strong networks of supporters in strategic places in the organization is a key factor for the sustainability of social innovations. All too often, we have seen the bold, pioneering work of intrapreneurs done over a period of years get unraveled in a few short months by the departure from the company of an important champion. Senior leaders like Jermyn Brooks in the PwC example, give vital coverage to more junior people who might otherwise be viewed as acting beyond their mandate by trying to create positive change. Upon the departure of CEO Jeff Kindler and his team from Pfizer, it was only a matter of months before the bold Access to Medicine initiative was wound down. Under Kindler, the initiative had top leadership support. When Kindler left, it made it more difficult for the intrapreneurs in the fledgling business unit to sustain a longer-term project to innovate new business models in emerging markets. Conversely, Accenture's Gib Bulloch gives credit to having been able to successfully transition his relationship with successive champions of his Accenture Development Partnerships model as a key to its enduring success and growth.

A couple of caveats are in order. First, although we have been portraying the process as one of essentially marketing an innovation, Kevin Thompson of IBM emphasized that an intrapreneur needs to balance planning and emergence. Few innovations are perfectly formed at the start, and the process of sharing and advocating can also be a process of serendipity that helps develop the innovation as well as accruing supporters. Be deliberate—but stay open.

Second, some innovations may not be compatible with a highly visible network of support. As we have described, domestic partner benefits were initially quite contentious, and many companies adopted them only after sustained efforts by internal social movements among their employees, as documented in research by Douglas Creed and Maureen Scully.[14] This activism was potentially quite risky. As of mid-2014, it was still legal in twenty-nine US states for employers to discriminate on the basis of sexual orientation. Indeed, there are instances in living memory of public corporations adopting HR policies explicitly seeking to purge LGBT employees.

Consider a thought experiment. A diabolical HR department in a company located in, say, Tennessee could set up a Facebook page called "Rainbow Alliance at Company X," gather a group of members—and then fire them all, perfectly legally. The point of this case is that visible activism can be risky for employees, and it is not always in everyone's best interest to have an explicit support network. We go into more detail about the risks of activism, online and off, in chapter 7.

The Nitty-Gritty: How to Analyze Network Data

After all that, you will be happy to learn that analyzing social network data is surprisingly easy today. Free software is readily available and fairly easy to use. Moreover, there are excellent recent books and online tutorials that can walk you through the essential steps of social network analysis. Here, we focus on a few easy steps to get at the major network concepts that we have described in this chapter.

We assume that you already have Excel installed on your computer and have basic familiarity with how it works. The first step is to download NodeXL, a free Excel plug-in. Although there are other softwares available for network analysis, NodeXL provides an easy and powerful entry point for budding network analysts. NodeXL (short for "network overview, discovery, and exploration for Excel") is a template that works with Excel to map network data. It produces excellent graphs (suitable for PowerPoint presentations) and allows extremely easy analysis.[a] With a bit of experience, a typical user can import, graph, and analyze social network data in under ten minutes. We have taught many classes of MBA students how to do this live, and they typically have a basic level of competence within two sessions. For a live case, we often have them use real data gathered from a survey of a thousand-plus employee company, and then explain their findings to company representatives in class the next day. (It is often an exercise in diplomacy as much as network analysis or presentation skills!)[b]

Next, we need to know how network data is formatted. The simplest way to get network data into NodeXL is to create a spreadsheet with two columns, where each row represents a relationship and the entry in each column is connected by that relationship. Suppose you asked a group of ten coworkers to name someone that they worked with on a daily basis. Andre names Beverly, Carol, and Diane. Beverly names Andre, Diane, Ed, and Garth. Carol names Andre, Diane, and Fernando.[c] And so on. The data would look like this:

Andre	Beverly
Andre	Carol
Andre	Diane
Beverly	Andre
Beverly	Diane
Beverly	Ed
Beverly	Garth
Carol	Andre
Carol	Diane
Carol	Fernando

Note that NodeXL calls a person or node a *vertex* and a relationship or tie an *edge*. (One of the peculiarities of social network

analysis is that everyone seems to have a different, specialized jargon.) After opening the NodeXL template, click on the tab at the bottom labeled "Edges," and copy and paste the two columns in under "Vertex1" and "Vertex2." Behind the scenes, NodeXL will turn this data into a matrix with each vertex listed as a row and column; the content of the cell shows the nature of the edge between the row person and the column person. To calculate a simple measure like degree, you can simply count the number of cells in a row that have something in them. Calculating more complicated measures like closeness require more sophisticated matrix operations.

To see a graph of the network, click the "Show Graph" button on the pane at the right. The graphics start simple but quickly become quite sophisticated. Interested readers are referred to an excellent guidebook, *Analyzing Social Media Networks with NodeXL: Insights from a Connected World,* written by the creators of NodeXL.

Finally, to calculate the most important measures we have described here, click on the "Graph Metrics" button, click "Select All," and go. NodeXL deposits all of the metrics calculated for each person in the "Vertices" tab.

In the appendix, we provide a quick guide to the most useful concepts discussed in this chapter and describe how to calculate them in NodeXL.

a. We highly recommend purchasing Derek Hansen, Ben Shneiderman, and Marc A. Smith, *Analyzing Social Media Networks with NodeXL: Insights from a Connected World* (Burlington, MA: Morgan Kaufmann, 2011).

b. You can find NodeXL and related resources at http://nodexl.codeplex.com/.

c. This example is provided by David Krackhardt at Carnegie-Mellon University. See http://www.orgnet.com/sna.html for a visualization.

Conclusion

Social network analysis allows us to take a few pieces of information, such as phone metadata, and assemble them into a surprisingly informative map. For those seeking to champion an innovation, knowing a few things about people's relationships—say, who e-mails whom over the course of a month, or who has worked together on common projects—can be enough to create a fairly precise map to show you where best to target your energies. Such information can also be used by those seeking to stifle innovation. This is one of the sources of concern around government collection of metadata. Although it may be reassuring to know that government spies are forbidden to listen in on our phone calls without court approval, it is alarming to discover just how much can be learned about us from simply tabulating who calls or e-mails whom.

Sociologist Kieran Healy wrote an ingenious piece for *Slate* describing what a British precursor to the NSA working for King George III might have learned from network analysis of metadata. By simply assembling and analyzing membership lists from independence-oriented groups (ye olde affiliation data), which included 254 individuals, it was possible to identify the most valuable anti-British terrorists targets to detain. The individual with the highest degree and betweenness scores? Paul Revere. Without knowing what was discussed at the meetings, it was evident that this was a person worth detaining before any trouble started.[15] In chapter 7, we see how far down that road many companies have gone.

CHAPTER SEVEN

How: Platforms for Mobilizing

In this chapter, we describe some of the potential benefits and hazards of different platforms for mobilization within organizations. Many observers argue that we have entered a new millennium for social movements and innovation due to advances in information and communication technologies. Since the turn of the twenty-first century, there have been a number of "pager revolutions," "text revolutions," "Facebook revolutions," and "Twitter revolutions." The most consequential have been the series of antiauthoritarian rebellions, starting in late 2010, that came to be called the Arab Spring.

Western commentators attributed much of the Arab Spring's potency and speed to social media. A focal point of Egypt's uprising was the Facebook page "We are all Khaled Said," which we described in chapter 5. The page was created by Google marketing executive Wael Ghonim after Said, a businessman in Alexandria, was dragged from an internet café and beaten to death by two plainclothes police in June 2010. The page, with graphic photos and videos documenting police brutality in Egypt, gathered 473,000 followers in the months leading up to the January protests in Cairo and evolved into a coordinating device for street protests. Shortly after the initial January 25 protests in Tahrir Square, security forces secretly imprisoned and questioned a blindfolded Ghonim for eleven days. Ultimately, of course, the Egyptian uprising was successful in ousting longtime dictator Hosni Mubarak rapidly and with relatively little bloodshed. In a subsequent interview on CNN, Ghonim stated: "I want to meet Mark Zuckerberg one day and thank him . . . This revolution started on Facebook . . . I always said that if you want to liberate a society, just give them the [internet]."[1]

In some sense, the uprisings in Tunisia, Egypt, Libya, and beyond were just what we should have expected. New technologies greatly lower the transaction costs of coordinated action. As Clay Shirky put it, "The centrality of group effort to human life means that anything that changes the way groups function will have profound ramifications for everything from commerce and government to media and religion . . . Most of the barriers to group action have collapsed, and without these barriers, we are free to explore new ways of gathering together and getting things done."[2] Online tools allow the very rapid spread of "sticky" information—going viral; they greatly increase the potential catchment area for participation; and they lower the threshold to join in. Those willing to show up in person in Tahrir Square and endure the risk of injury or death for the cause can do so (and even use Google Maps to find the quickest route in and potential escape routes out). Those who prefer to engage in online activism, or who have skills in writing programs to work around government constraints, can contribute that way.

But the same tools used by activists can also be used by those seeking to crush them. An investigative series by Bloomberg in 2011 titled "Wired for Repression" revealed that many Western electronics and telecom companies had provided equipment and tools to repressive Middle Eastern regimes that used them to monitor their populace, including phone tapping, text retrieval, and location tracking for mobile phones.[3]

Street protests broke out for days in Tehran in the wake of Iran's corrupt elections in June 2009. Activists relied heavily on text messages to spread the word—evidently unaware that their messages and location were tracked by "lawful interception" technologies sold and installed by Western companies. One protestor—ironically, an Ericsson employee—was beaten, jailed for fifty-two days, and interrogated more than a dozen times by security agents who showed him data that had been collected on his location at various times leading up to the protest, transcripts of his text messages, and a two-step network diagram showing the people he had called and the people *they* had called. In these circumstances, seemingly innocent choices such as whom to friend on Facebook can have profound consequences.[4]

More recent revelations show that Iran is not the only country to keep track of the locations, phone records, and social networks of their citizens. A spoof in the *Onion* suggesting that Facebook was actually an elaborate CIA surveillance tool turned out to be not so far from the truth.[5] And while most corporate employers are a bit more open than the government of Iran under Ahmadinejad, many of the biggest companies have their own technologies for keeping track of their human resources. These can range from the mundane (GPS trackers on company vehicles) to the Orwellian ("sentiment analysis" of the texts of employee e-mails, which analyzes the emotional tone of messages based on the phrases used).

People can mobilize in any number of ways and in any number of places, from the bowling alley to the boardroom. Here, we are particularly interested in the promise and perils of online mobilizing technologies. We write mindful of the potential risks associated with social intrapreneurship, and note the tradeoffs of different kinds of mobilizing structures.

What Are Mobilizing Structures?

Mobilizing structures are the organizing devices through which people get involved in innovations or movements. Several years ago, political scientist Robert Putnam wrote about the decline in the social institutions that had knit together American communities in a book titled *Bowling Alone*. His argument was that bowling leagues, PTAs, labor unions, fraternal organizations, and other groupings that brought people together face-to-face on a regular basis helped create cohesion among members of communities, which enabled them to act collectively toward common goals. The decline of these connecting organizations, he argued, was associated with a decline in civic engagement. Joiners tend to be voters who care about school board elections; non-joiners, less so.[6]

From his prior work on democratic reforms in Italy, Putnam had determined that the social networks created by, say, choral societies were good for democracy and good for business. Regular meetings made it possible to alert people to new developments, raise issues that required attention, and sometimes resolve to do something about them.

Much the same is true in the business world. Cities where the top business executives are well connected with each other are much more effective at getting things done as a group than dispersed cities. The twin cities of Minneapolis–St. Paul are renowned for the generosity of their locally headquartered companies and, thanks to well-funded local arts organizations, have a vibrant cultural life as a result. The folklore among executive recruiters is that Minneapolis is one of the hardest places to recruit *to,* because of the weather, and one of the hardest places to recruit *from,* because of the quality of life once you get there.

How do they do it? In large part, though strong norms of civic engagement that are enforced by a dense social network, in which local CEOs serve on each other's boards and on those of the same cultural institutions, such as the Walker Art Center. If a CEO fails to contribute to this year's fund drive, his or her colleagues are likely to point it out after the next board meeting. Much the same goes for Atlanta, where for years the CEOs of Coca-Cola, UPS, Home Depot, SunTrust Banks, Georgia Power, and other local businesses have met regularly on the same corporate boards. According to Boston College's Mary Ann Glynn, this was one of the factors that made Atlanta's business community so effective in their bid for the Olympics.[7]

In any given social system, such as an organization, there is some level of latent support for innovation and change. Mobilizing structures can turn that potential energy into actual energy. IBM's Kevin Thompson found that the company blog was the equivalent of the early political pamphlets as a way of getting out the story of the Corporate Service Corps to Big Blue's 400,000 employee population. Once people knew about the idea, it resonated with them as something new and different. Given how globally disparate the employee population is—Thompson himself works mostly from a home office in Dexter, Michigan—it was inevitable that the appropriate mobilizing structure would be online. In this remote working context, and at a time of tight budgets, Thompson found he was able to form a team of forty people each working two hours a week toward his initiative much easier than he could get approval for two new full-time hires. In the American civil rights movement, on the other hand, one of the most important mobilizing structures was the network of black churches in the South. As Aldon Morris of Northwestern University has shown, the churches provided leadership, resources, a locus for recruitment, a safe place for meetings, and a dense communication network for the diffusion of information and tactics through personal connections, ministerial alliances, and ties to local colleges. The churches became, in Morris's terms, local movement centers.[8]

Mobilizing structures provide a platform for innovators and movements to launch actions toward their goals. Consider one of the characteristic forms of protest of the civil rights movement: the sit-in. Before the Civil Rights Act of 1965 was passed, it was legal and quite common for businesses in the American South, including hotels, restaurants, and stores, to maintain racially segregated facilities. In sit-ins, African Americans occupied segregated facilities to draw attention to injustice. The sit-in was explicitly nonviolent, and protestors did not respond to provocations with violence or property damage; they simply resisted passively, following the examples of Mohandas Gandhi and Martin Luther King.

The most famous sit-in took place on the afternoon of February 1, 1960, when four local black college students seated themselves at the segregated lunch counter of a Woolworth's store in Greensboro, North Carolina. They were refused service, but remained until the store closed. The next day, roughly twenty black students returned to sit, unserved, at the counter, this time attracting press attention. The next day, more than sixty protestors showed up; the day after that, over three hundred. The sit-in was accompanied by a highly successful boycott. Within two months, sit-ins had taken place at stores in dozens of cities across the South, drawing international attention to the widespread legal segregation in the United States. As Aldon Morris discovered, the sit-in had been developed and refined over prior years and drew on the support of local black churches to provide training, support, bail money, and legal counsel. Through dense ties between churches, the sit-in rapidly diffused and became an iconic tactic of the movement.[9]

Scholars of social movements use the term *collective action repertoires* to describe the most typical formats for group action in a specific setting. During the American Revolution, pamphlets were a preferred means of spreading ideas, and typical forms of activism included petitions, hanging in effigy, and tarring and feathering of tax collectors. In Paris, in contrast, popular protests almost inevitably involved tearing up the streets to build barricades out of the paving stones. (Indeed, one of the goals of administrator and planner Baron Haussmann's "urban renewal" of Paris in the mid-1800s was to create boulevards wide enough to prevent their blockage and allow troops to pass through in the event of civil unrest.[10])

The sit-in was well suited to the civil rights movement because merely by sitting peacefully at a lunch counter, protestors were violating the law, thereby dramatizing the law's injustice and absurdity. Moreover, college students typically have the unencumbered time and absence of outside commitments (families, jobs) that make risky activism unpalatable for older adults. The sit-in was a perfect protest tactic for this movement at this moment in history.

Information Technology and Mobilizing Structures

In the past few decades, the range of formats for group action has expanded tremendously thanks to new technology.[11] Flash mobs are an example. These are groups that converge at a particular time and place for a particular activity, usually organized over the Web or by mobile phones. Flash mobs initially began whimsically, with groups convening to dance or participate in elaborate mini-dramas. Within a few years, the form had been adapted for less benign uses. In Philadelphia in early 2010, flash mobs of bored teenagers began to turn violent, leading the city to impose a curfew. In August 2011, flash mobs across the United Kingdom took the form of coordinated looting in town centers. Savvy organizers avoided Facebook and Twitter, using BlackBerry Messenger (BBM) texts forwarded to trusted friends instead. Unlike social media, BBM is encrypted and thus more difficult for the authorities to track. Ironically, social media such as Facebook, YouTube, and Flickr hosted photos and videos taken by participants and observers of the riots that enabled the police to identify and arrest participants afterward.

Virtual protests are an example of what sociologist Jennifer Earl calls *e-movements*.[12] As we saw in chapter 3, three days after the Susan G. Komen For the Cure foundation cut off funding for breast cancer screenings for low-income women at Planned Parenthood, a massive virtual movement forced it to reverse course, but not before seriously damaging its reputation. Remarkably, the entire protest had happened virtually, and nearly anonymously.

Even the venerable March on Washington has taken on a new cast. The US Chamber of Commerce protested financial regulations pending in Congress in 2010 by launching a "virtual march on Washington" comprising over twenty-four thousand online avatars gathered on a Google map of the National Mall. The avatars were labeled and organized by geography to demonstrate small business opposition to the bill.[13]

We can attribute some of these new forms of group action to the affordances of the technology. *Affordances*—the way a system or tool such as software is organized or formatted—can shape the form of collective action. For instance, Facebook is useful for enrolling and aggregating members. When you create a page, as Wael Ghonim did, you can gather likes and friends to assess the extent of sympathy for a cause and share photos and links to other information. This is good for enrolling a large group of dispersed allies. Twitter allows users to re-tweet prior postings that they find relevant, thus amplifying a message. This is good for rapidly "pushing" news to those that might use it. Blackberry Messenger (BBM) is good for sending secure messages to selected others. This is effective for messages intended to stay under the radar.

By increasing routine access to friends and colleagues, social media makes it easier to be exposed to their attitudes. In the literature on diffusion of innovation, innovations diffuse faster when they are visible. Wearing a baseball cap backward, or a black North Face fleece, can spread very quickly within communities and became nearly universal, as those who live in the vicinity of college undergrads can attest. Attitudes, on the other hand—such as support for change—are not usually so overt.

Social media makes it possible for opinions that might otherwise be invisible to spread in the same way as fashions. For instance, in March 2013, as the US Supreme Court was deciding on the constitutionality of the Defense of Marriage Act (prohibiting federal recognition of same-sex marriage), the Human Rights Campaign encouraged Facebook users to change their profile picture to a pink equal sign to signify support for marriage equality. It was the kind of meme that could spread almost instantly as millions joined the bandwagon, and many people's newsfeeds became a sea of pink equality symbols (or clever variations).

We should expect to see that different affordances are associated with different kinds of collective action. On January 18, 2012, in a protest against the proposed Stop Online Piracy Act (SOPA) in the US Congress, Wikipedia shut down its English-language services for a day and turned its home page a stark black, featuring information about why it opposed SOPA. Wikipedia was joined by Google, Reddit, and over 100,000 other websites in partially or completely shutting down that day. Twenty years earlier, such a "web page strike" would have been not just impossible, but literally inconceivable. The strike was highly successful in peeling away support for the bill, which was shelved.[14]

Lessons from the Arab Spring

The history of the Arab Spring provides a brief tutorial in the possibilities provided by contemporary technology. The initial spark was ignited in Tunisia. Mohamed Bouazizi, a street vendor, sold fruits and vegetables bought on credit in an illegal street stall to support his extended family. Policewoman Faida Hamdy seized his goods and, when he protested, allegedly slapped him across the face in view of the public. Robbed of his dignity and no longer able to provide for his family, Bouazizi appeared in front of the governor's office, doused himself with paint thinner, and lit a match. He died in the hospital on January 4, 2011.

Self-immolation in a provincial capital does not generally attract much attention; indeed, the act is far more common than one would guess. In this case, however, a Facebook page commemorating Bouazizi set up by a freelance journalist attracted a series of amateur cell phone video postings documenting conditions in Tunisia. These were then broadcast on Al Jazeera, the global cable news channel centered in Qatar. The broadcasts in turn yielded more video posts, which received more air time. The attention from Al Jazeera prompted massive street protests in Tunisia that were viewed around the world. Within nine days of Bouazizi's death, the movement ended the autocratic twenty-three-year reign of dictator Zine al-Abidine Ben Ali—a remarkable and unprecedented event.

Activists in Tunisia had also been in contact with their counterparts in Egypt—over Facebook, naturally. Cross-national ties between activists were used to share methods and targets of nonviolent protest, drawing on the writings of Gene Sharp—who had inspired prior activists in Serbia and elsewhere.[15] Facebook was also used to spread specific tactics, such as dipping bandanas in vinegar to deal with tear gas, using milk to flush out afflicted eyes, and taping together empty plastic bottles under baggy shirts to act as armor against police batons.

The Facebook page that provided a focal point for internet-savvy activists in Egypt, "We are all Khaled Said," proclaimed

January 25 as a day for protest. Drawing on the affordances of Facebook, it polled users to ask what color of clothing to wear for silent protests, as the "color revolutions" in various countries had shown this to be an effective way to highlight support without overt confrontation. The page also sought pre-commitment from at least fifty thousand members to verify that a sufficiently large protest on January 25 would come off. Facebook and YouTube served as repositories for how-to videos for nonviolent resistance, as well as cannier advice (such as spray-painting police windshields and disabling their vehicles by blocking exhaust pipes).[16]

Egypt showed that governments were not powerless in the face of the Web. On January 28, three days after the initiating protests in Tahrir Square, the government of Egypt essentially cut the country off from the internet and instructed mobile phone providers to shut down service. Like many Middle Eastern countries, Egypt owns the "pipes" that carry internet and phone traffic, and had the ability to sever connections to the outside world. Because many of the essential functions that people use, such as e-mail and domain name directories, are housed on servers outside the country, cutting these connections largely crippled the internal internet as well. Although internet and phone service returned within days, Egypt had demonstrated that the "cyber-utopians" (as Evgeny Morozov calls them) who view the internet as an intrinsically democratizing technology were far too optimistic.[17] When states perceive that their security is at risk, they can be quite agile in controlling the technology.

On the other hand, the conceptual architecture of the internet makes it possible to create secure local networks outside of the purview of governments and intrusive telecom companies.

Low cost "mesh networks" have been created in neighborhoods in Greece, Latin America, and even Detroit by combining satellite connections to the broader internet with inexpensive Wi-Fi hardware attached to users' computers to build a local web. As a bonus, these networks can evade governmental filters and surveillance. Similar methods allow people to create a highly localized mobile phone network using the phones' own Bluetooth signals. This can act like a fancy walkie-talkie system, cutting out the telecoms. The New America Foundation's Open Technology Institute created "Commotion Wireless" as a set of open-source software tools and documentation to allow activists or others to build their own wireless communication network on the ground, potentially rendering efforts to "turn off the internet" futile.[18] It is clear that connective technologies will generate a perpetual arms race between activists and those seeking to stop them, and it is impossible to predict where things will end up.

Lessons for Intrapreneurs from Social Movements

What can social innovators learn from the civil rights movement and the Arab Spring? First, mobilizing structures can be low-tech but highly effective. Black churches in the South led by progressive ministers were a remarkably powerful backbone of the civil rights movement. Regular but informal encounters at the coffee machine can provide a means for recruiting allies for innovation. Affinity groups based on common background (e.g., ethnicity, alumni ties) also often serve as launchpads for common action. Connective technologies might be thought of as accelerators rather than replacements for more traditional face-to-face ties. Indeed, some workplaces ban social networking on company computers, meaning that more traditional organizing methods often gain more traction.

Second, these tools evolve so rapidly that it is futile to make specific predictions or recommendations about the best software platform. Clay Shirky noted that when he started writing his best-selling book *Here Comes Everybody*, Twitter did not exist. By the time a draft was completed, Twitter had millions of users around the world and had become a common platform for collective action. The first iPhone was released in June 2007, at which point Nokia and BlackBerry were dominant players in the consumer and professional mobile phone markets. Today, smartphones with Wi-Fi internet access, video cameras, and GPS are ubiquitous; Nokia and BlackBerry are mere echoes of their former selves; and Google Glass is on the horizon as a potential category-changing alternative. Nevertheless, we can point to some of the features of technology to look for, drawing on recent experience.

Third, we must recognize that there are strong reasons to be cautious about using connective technologies within companies. When it comes to high-tech monitoring of what goes on inside their borders, government agencies in Iran and Egypt have nothing on HR and IT departments in the corporate world. Recognize that your corporate e-mail account, intranet, and company-provided phone are owned by (and open to) the company.

There are certainly sensible legal reasons for companies to monitor their employees' online activities. *The Economist* described e-discovery firms that specialize in using software analysis of corporate e-mail to uncover signs of fraud or conspiracy—something of great interest to top management:

> *Cataphora's software lets firms analyse everything from e-mails to electronic calendars and thus build a picture of typical patterns of communication across their operations. It then flags exceptions to those patterns, such as individuals who send many messages to one another even though they are not in the same unit and have little reason to interact . . . The software can dig deeper still by analysing linguistic patterns. In one case, Cataphora spotted a link between several executives at a firm that had been issuing bogus invoices to inflate its revenues. A program flagged that the executives, who were all in on the scam, had been using the same unusual sign-off phrase in their e-mails, which turned out to be associated with a college fraternity to which they had all belonged.*[19]

In short, employees who seek to break down corporate silos and collaborate across boundaries using the company e-mail system—say, fraudsters or social intrapreneurs—might well find themselves getting a closer look. Indeed, Chris was due to teach a workshop on network analysis to future top executives at a *Fortune* 50 company on the same day that the NSA metadata collection scandal broke. Suffice it to say, the group was very ready for a conversation on the ethics of surveillance techniques such as e-mail monitoring that day.

IBM goes further with a tool called IBM Security Intelligence with Big Data, which can use sentiment analysis (mentioned earlier in this chapter) to detect differences in the tone of employee's e-mails and social media use. An article in the *Wall Street Journal* described potential uses of this tool: "For example, a company could analyze employee e-mails that express a positive sentiment to a manager at work, but detect 'when he's talking to a peer or someone outside the company, the sentiment comes out a little different,' [an IBM representative] said. Such a pattern, combined with other factors, could cause an employee to be flagged for more investigation by an IT team." Notably, this tool is not limited to internal corporate e-mail and transactions but draws on postings on public social media.[20]

At a somewhat less intrusive level, many companies have strict limits on what kinds of information technology can be used at the office or on company computers. Facebook, Skype, LinkedIn, and other common tools for connecting may not be practically accessible. This means that employees may need to go outside the company's own IT system to organize.

One of the most intriguing examples of company employees using websites outside the company to create organizational change happened at HealthSouth. HealthSouth became one of the largest chains of rehabilitation hospitals and services in the United States through a series of acquisitions led by its founder and CEO, Richard Scrushy, and encouraged by fee-hungry investment banks. During Scrushy's tenure, the company accumulated a sizeable air force of corporate jets, luxury cars, and a lavish corporate headquarters with a private executive elevator and sponsored a country music band in which Scrushy played. Along the way, employees began to notice accounting irregularities and questioned the earnings figures HealthSouth was reporting. Some of them went public with their concerns in an unconventional forum: the Yahoo Finance web page dedicated to HealthSouth's stock. Their insider details provoked questions and concerns from other investors; their accusations against Scrushy, on the other hand, provoked legal action by HealthSouth and Scrushy, including a subpoena of Yahoo that exposed the identities of the anonymous posters. The fraud at HealthSouth continued for several years until a former accountant at the company also blew the whistle via Yahoo Finance posts. Although Scrushy eventually did prison time for an unrelated crime and faced a multibillion-dollar civil judgment for fraud at HealthSouth, the case shows that anonymous e-whistleblowing may not stay anonymous.[21]

The upshot of all this is that public sites are not the best bet for organizing your intrapreneurial venture. Assume that your online activities can and will be monitored by your employer.

Finding the Right Tools for Mobilization

The dilemma we have highlighted in this chapter is this: on the one hand, new technologies dramatically lower the cost and expand the range of possibilities for group action. On the other, companies are increasingly savvy about tracking employee activities on the company e-mail server and internal network and on external sites.

Our first piece of advice is to choose your tools carefully. The ideal mobilizing tool allows an innovator to recruit allies, gather and share information, poll members for preferences, collaborate on work, and push news out to those who need it. At the same time, it is extremely useful to be able to do this under the radar, avoiding the corporate antibodies before the innovation has had a chance to gestate. Tools that do not require installing software, and particularly those that can be used on smartphones, are therefore particularly attractive.

Our second piece of advice is to avoid investing too much in any particular information and communication technologies (ICT) tool. In our course, we brought in a guest speaker with substantial experience in online collaboration tools to advise our class on good bets. Eighteen months later, all but one of the sites he recommended had shut down; moreover, one of the two omnibus review sites intended to provide guidance on what tools to choose had closed. Thus, we are wary of advising anyone to go all-in on an ICT that might turn out to fade like Friendster or MySpace, and instead leave it to your best judgment. The technologies we reference in this book, whether in depth or by way of example, will most likely be superseded by new and better resources before long. However, the need to time your initiative, make the case, know your network, and organize appropriately will remain—and tools will be helpful to you to that end.

Two tools we have had good experiences with that are likely to be reasonably long-lived are Ning and Yammer. Ning is a platform for creating private social networks—like Facebook, but for groups united by a common interest. An attractive feature of Ning is that it has an intuitively familiar interface, is low-cost or free, and can be set up to require that new members be admitted by permission. Yammer is intended for within-company social networks, and thus less under the radar than Ning, but it allows for the creation of groups by invitation. Users are able to share files and work on common documents, and as a format for collaboration, Ning allows users to avoid the glut of "reply all" messages that are the bane of e-mail conversations.

Conclusion

Information and communication technologies have dramatically changed the possibilities for coordinating group action. Mobilizing dispersed groups for purposes from meetings to flash mobs to revolutions has never been easier. One result of this is that we are seeing much more frequent mobilization for social change, from the small scale (the relentless online petitions for various causes around the world; the rapid micro-movements in response to consumer complaints such as price increases in mobile phone plans) to the societal (the Tea Party and Occupy in the United States; the Arab Spring in the Middle East). It is inevitable that this will change how social and other innovations are done at the organizational level. For the moment, corporations often lean toward a more locked-down approach to IT that makes online mobilization for social innovation within organizations risky. The Arab Spring would never have taken off in most corporate settings. Yet there are signs of movement toward a "bring your own device" approach, particularly among millennials, that will enable a new wave of social innovation. We can't point to specific software tools that are immune from becoming obsolete—recent history suggests that relentless innovation would make any suggestions quaint by the time the paperback edition came out. But we can say that smart companies will be those that enable the progress of social innovation rather than sending in teams from IT and HR to quash it.

CHAPTER EIGHT

Change Your Company, Change the World

When we started teaching social intrapreneurship in 2010, there had been no Arab Spring. Corporate movements were sporadic, things like occasional boycotts against Nestlé or Nike. The possibilities for technology-enabled activism were just beginning to be realized on a large scale. These days, owing to the declining costs of organizing collectively, social movements seem to be everywhere.

Thanks in part to smartphones and the Web, movements for social change are becoming a pervasive feature of contemporary society, including the business world. Increasingly ubiquitous video cameras, GPS, and web connectivity greatly enhance the prospects for movements to arise and scale rapidly.

Companies cannot easily opt out of this climate. As we described in chapter 1, Starbucks tried to avoid controversy around gun rights by simply following local laws on "open carry." Yet in August 2013, the company found itself the unwilling beneficiary of "Starbucks Appreciation Day" rallies by thousands of customers brandishing weapons, forcing it to take a stand that would inevitably be construed harshly by one side or another.

Another example from chapter 1—Mozilla promoted one of its founders to CEO in March 2014, only to accept his resignation two weeks later, not because of concerns about his technical competence, but because of his opposition to gay marriage, which had prompted a spontaneous movement against his appointment inside and outside the company.

Facebook, Twitter, and other social media allow opinions on social issues to be expressed and aggregated with minimal cost. If customers, employees, or other stakeholders have a strong opinion on a company's actions, chances are good that it will be heard.

Some companies have begun to harness the new technologies of social movements. Airbnb, the online service that allows people to rent out rooms in their homes as an alternative to hotels, responded to investigations by New York's attorney general of potential violations of rental regulations by posting an online petition at Peers.org to "protect all New Yorkers," not just big hotels, and to "support the sharing economy." The petition's sponsor stated that "Many people are struggling in today's economy and people like me depend on Airbnb to pay the mortgage and keep the lights on . . . For many of us, Airbnb is the only thing that keeps us in the homes we love." The petition had twenty thousand signatures within a day.[1]

As the stories in this book have shown, social innovations in companies are frequently the result of internal social movements by employees. From new triple-bottom-line products and services to the creation of human rights codes, initiatives often result from social intrapreneurs leading a movement among their colleagues. Intrapreneurs can be a bridge connecting social change in the world to resources within the company. Successful intrapreneurs manage to persuade both colleagues and management that their idea is worth pursuing, and fits with the company's priorities.

In many companies, the default setting is to quash social innovations, letting the corporate antibodies prevent them from taking hold. Yet smart businesses will be adaptable to social change by creating a climate that is open to such social innovation movements. If social change is inevitable, then it makes sense for firms to create mechanisms to adapt rather than be left behind.

In this final chapter, we describe how some companies have managed to thrive by being open to internal social innovations. We conclude by pointing out how change can be contagious, for the better.

Creating an Adaptable Organization

Throughout this book, we have described social innovations and their champions. Our aim was to give guidance to intrapreneurs—those working in the trenches. But to this point, we have been less concerned with the view from the top. What is it that makes some companies more fertile climates for social innovation? Is it industry, demography, culture, or something else? And can it be learned?

We have found that some human capital–intensive industries are more inherently receptive to social innovation than others.

Accounting and consulting firms are often highly responsive to the social demands of their employees. The interns at PricewaterhouseCoopers that championed a social audit practice (see chapter 6) are just one example of many we heard from the accounting industry. We also found that the professionals we spoke with at Accenture, in offices on three continents, consistently lauded the firm for its willingness to support innovations, from Gib Bulloch's Accenture Development Partnerships to professional programs for First Peoples in Canada and support for call centers in native communities. This fits with the idea that much innovation is driven by a war for talent. Businesses that require professionals with skills in high demand are virtually required to embrace the preferences of the next generation. Woe to the recruiting company that fails to have HR practices that honor diversity.

Firms with a strong brand to protect are also often social innovators receptive to intrapreneurs. Nike faced consumer backlash in the 1990s when malign labor practices in some of its suppliers became widely known. Perhaps most notable was a story in *Life* magazine that included a photo of a Pakistani child sewing Nike-branded soccer balls, titled "Six cents an hour."[2] Protests and calls for boycotts put Nike in the center of battles around globalization.

The firm subsequently became an innovator in supply chain accountability and promulgated a rigorous supplier code of conducts, accompanied by third-party factory inspections. In early 2013, when factory conditions in Bangladesh came to light, Nike cut ties to some suppliers in Bangladesh whose factories were deemed unsafe—even at the expense of its margins and in the face of declining profitability relative to competitors. Internal advocates for safety and labor rights in the supply chain have become powerful contenders within Nike. Because of its light footprint in Bangladesh, Nike was not among the Western brands implicated in the tragic factory collapse in Dhaka in April of that year.[3]

Yet we found welcoming environments for social innovation in firms operating in quite diverse industries. In consumer packaged goods, SC Johnson has sourced raw materials from farmers in Rwanda, partnered with local providers to improve hygiene and sanitation in low-income urban communities in Kenya, and chosen to eliminate harmful chemicals from its production processes in spite of the negative consequences for its market share. In retail, Whole Foods has eliminated plastic bags, worked to develop local suppliers, and opened stores with affordable products in low-income communities with limited access to fresh produce. Cascade Engineering evolved from an industrial supplier to the auto industry to Michigan's first certified B corporation, spawning a broad array of innovations from employee management (the Welfare-to-Career program described in chapter 2) to products such as the Hydraid BioSand Water Filter, a high-capacity, low-cost household water filter aimed at low-income countries. These innovations often emerged from employee-generated ideas and even through employee-led initiatives.

Our observation is that the key to creating a climate for social innovation is not the industry but the culture of the organization and the commitment of top management.

We have also seen how a change at the top can be transformative for social innovation within companies. When William Clay Ford Jr. took over as chairman of Ford, it signaled that the nearly century-old firm was open to change, from its environmental initiatives to its award-winning programs to combat HIV/AIDS in South Africa to its global Human Rights Code.

Yet new leaders do not have to have their family name on the door to enable social innovation. In 2003, when Rámon de Mendiola took over as CEO of Florida Ice & Farm Company, Costa Rica's leading beer and beverage producer, the firm was an old-fashioned and complacent incumbent facing imminent competition from world-class global competitors. Mendiola launched a campaign to increase efficiency and cut costs, followed by another campaign to introduce new products and increase revenues and profits, culminating in the acquisition of the PepsiCo business in Costa Rica. After building credibility inside and outside the organization, in 2008 Mendiola created a broad initiative to remake Florida as a triple-bottom-line business devoted to profit, planet, and people. He stated that most businesses are caterpillars that eat and eat; he wanted Florida to be a butterfly, which enchants and pollinates, combining business performance with social progress. The company committed to goals of being water neutral by 2012, carbon neutral by 2017, and ultimately zero waste. Its people initiatives included aggressive targets for employee volunteerism, partnering with Habitat for Humanity to build housing in the wake of an earthquake in 2009 and building facilities to provide fresh water access for villages in rural areas of Costa Rica. The company's culture has had a number of tangible benefits, including increased employee loyalty and retention and, intriguingly, goodwill from potential acquisition targets, whose owners can rest easy in handing their businesses over to a company with a strong commitment to the triple bottom line.

The most recent product of this approach is YES Florida, a social business collaboration between Florida Ice & Farm and the Yunus Centre run by Muhammad Yunus. The goal of the business is to address problems of malnutrition facing children from gestation to two years old, where iron deficiency is particularly problematic. In response, Florida developed low-cost fortified infant cereals and fortified instant soups that are ready to eat and high in nutrition. The foods would be primarily distributed by a network of community saleswomen, thereby creating employment opportunities. The alliance's explicit objective is to reduce poverty and undernutrition, not to maximize profit, although the business is designed to be economically sustainable.[4]

The point of this discussion is that there are plenty of examples of businesses that adopt a triple bottom line and manage to be both economically and socially sustainable, and to encourage grassroots social innovation. Perhaps the coming generation of leaders will come to embrace this approach as Ramón de Mendiola did, with similar results.

Change Can Be Contagious

Significant changes often do not stay bottled up in organizations, but spread from company to company through a kind of contagion process. In the mid-1980s, a handful of corporate boards adopted "poison pill" defenses that were invented by clever lawyers and proved to be highly effective at warding off unwanted hostile takeovers. At the time, it was not unusual for boards to have directors in common. In fact, the average *Fortune* 500 company's directors served on nine additional boards, and some companies such as banks shared directors with dozens of others. Well-connected directors were instrumental in spreading the poison pill. As they went from board meeting to board meeting, they shared their positive assessments of the pill with their colleagues (in spite of the strong opposition of institutional investors), and within eighteen months, more than half of the *Fortune* 500 had adopted a poison pill.[5] Similar stories can be told for many corporate practices, from total quality management to the creation of investor relations offices.

There are many networks that can promote the contagion of corporate practices. When founders or other personnel move from one firm to another, they often import practices, creating family resemblances. The many progeny of Fairchild Semiconductor in Silicon Valley are a famous example. Membership in professional associations connects firms to best practices; for example, in human resource management. Industry benchmarking holds out exemplars for companies to emulate. Codes of conduct for suppliers allow large firms to dictate practices to their dependent suppliers. Even simple geographic proximity can act to diffuse ideas and practices. Employee learn what their friends are earning, what they're working on, new programs, and so on; soon, everybody has a foosball table.

All of these networks create a corporate system that is susceptible to contagion, for better or worse. The implication is that a change in one organization can be like tipping the first domino. By showing "proof of concept," change in one company becomes available to other activists to advocate for.

Domestic partner benefits provide an example that is by now familiar. They were first adopted in peripheral firms, were picked up by Lotus in the early 1990s, spread fitfully over the next decade, and received a big boost from their adoption by the Big Three automakers in 1999. By 2013, even Walmart had adopted them. Such benefits had become part of the standard employment package, arousing little of the controversy that first greeted them. Perhaps less obvious is how activists inside companies used adoption by peers as a rhetorical resource. The ability to approach the CEO or head of HR with a list of "benchmark" companies that had already done something turns out to be quite powerful, particularly when failing to do so erodes the firm's ability to recruit.

Yet change is not inevitably contagious. Plenty of worthy ideas fail to catch on, just as wheeled luggage gained only limited acceptance in the first twenty years after its invention. Consider the fight against HIV/AIDS. In January 2001, UN Secretary General Kofi Annan made a speech to the US Chamber of Commerce urging business leaders to join the global fight against HIV/AIDS, particularly in sub-Saharan Africa, where government resources were stretched to their limit:

> *I come to you, the leaders of American business, representatives of one of the greatest forces in the world, but one which has yet to be fully utilized in the campaign against AIDS/HIV. It is high time we tapped your strengths to the full . . . Business is used to acting decisively and quickly. The same cannot be said of the community of sovereign states. We need your help—right now . . . Together, I believe we can succeed—if only because the costs of failure are simply too appalling to contemplate.[6]*

He endorsed the Global Business Coalition on HIV/AIDS (GBC) as the preferred vehicle to join the fight: it was inexpensive (only $25,000 per company to join) and was run by Richard Holbrooke, a man highly respected in business and policy circles.

Yet a few years later, only two dozen members of the *Fortune* 500 had joined the GBC. The pattern of contagion was intriguing: every firm with an African American CEO—Time Warner, American Express, Merrill Lynch, and Fannie Mae— joined the GBC, as did virtually every firm on whose board these CEOs served. Yet surprisingly enough, membership did not become contagious the way that the poison pill did, suggesting that only some innovations are likely to go viral.

As we have seen, many innovations go from crazy, to innovative, to best practice, to standard. Yet this pathway is not inevitable, and it requires individual innovators to keep the momentum going. We hope this book has provided useful guidance on how to make that happen.

Mapping Networks with NodeXL

A Quick Guide to Using NodeXL

Here is a step-by-step guide to doing your own analysis using free software.

1. Download NodeXL, which is an open source Excel-based add-on for basic network analysis. From the main website (http://nodexl.codeplex.com/), go to "Downloads" and download the latest version to your desktop and install it. The installation creates a shortcut to an Excel template with the set of macros necessary to set up a data sheet and run analyses.

2. Open the Excel template by clicking on the shortcut in your Start menu. You get to an empty version of the Excel template (see figure A-1):

3. From here, you can either import network data, for example from your Outlook e-mails, or enter data manually. Switch to the NodeXL tab in Excel to access

FIGURE A-1

NodeXL template

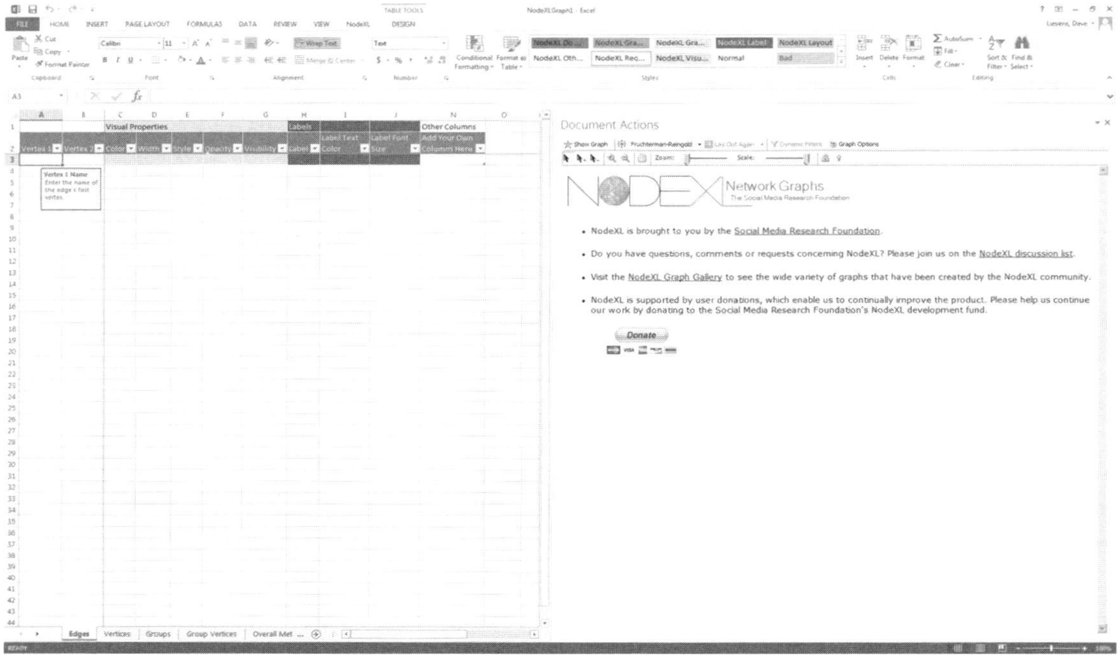

the menu. A note about terminology: NodeXL uses the technical terms of network analysis. It calls individuals *vertices* and relationships *edges*. So enter new people in the tab "Vertices" and new relationships in the tab "Edges." (See the glossary at the end of this appendix.)

4. Click on the "Show Graph" button in the Graph window. This will give you a simple network diagram that can be suitably accessorized once you have some practice.

5. You can play around with the layout a bit by manually dragging individuals around. A first piece of information you can glean from the graph is how dense your network is: Is everyone else around you connected to each other or are you communicating with separate groups? This gives you some sense of how much of a broker you are.

6. You can also click on any of the individuals to see who that person is. The person's identifier is highlighted in the "Vertices" tab and his or her relationships are marked in red in the graph. Particularly interesting are individuals who connect you to many others (the brokers you rely on), those that connect otherwise dis-connected groups in your networks (brokers that "com-pete" with you for connecting groups), and "thick" ties that reflect closer ties.

7. You can also calculate several of the individual and network statistics discussed above, including different measures of individual centrality: cliques, density, and centralization. Use the menu to do so: *NodeXL>GraphMetrics>* and check the boxes of the measures you want to create.

Glossary of Network Terms with Special Reference to NodeXL

Attribute	A characteristic of a person, such as age, education, sex, department, or other background characteristics. *In NodeXL: Attributes appear on the "Vertices" tab and can be used to change the appearance of nodes.*
Type of tie	The *content* of a connection, such as informal socializing, advice, collaboration, or trust.
Strength of tie	The *quantity or quality* of a relationship, such as frequency of communication. *In NodeXL: represented by "Edge Weight" on the "Edges" tab (e.g., number of directors shared by two corporate boards).*
Tie direction	The point toward which something flows or moves, such as advice giving (often indicated by arrowheads in a network diagram). *In NodeXL: When you draw a graph, ties between nodes can be asymmetric (one arrowhead) or symmetric (two arrowheads).*
Distance	The fewest number of links between two people in a network; also called *path distance* or *geodesic*.
Centrality	The extent to which a person is connected. Different ways of measuring this include: **Degree:** The simple number of contacts (e.g., how many friends you have) **In-degree:** The number of times you are a *target* of a relation (e.g., how many people seek you for advice) **Out-degree:** The number of times you are a *sender* of a relation (e.g., how many people you seek for advice) **Closeness:** How few "steps" or "degrees" it takes to reach everyone else; can also be measured as average distance (the average "shortest path" to everyone else in the network) **Betweenness:** The number of times you are on the shortest path (geodesic) between every other pair of nodes in the network **Eigenvector:** Similar to Google's PageRank, it measures the extent to which those you are connected to are themselves well connected *In NodeXL: individual degree, closeness, betweenness, and eigenvector centrality are calculated by clicking* Graph Metrics>Select All>Calculate Metrics *and deposited on the "Vertices" tab.*

Density   The proportion of realized ties, expressed as a percent of maximum number possible (n[n-1]/2); density varies between 0% and 100%

In NodeXL: see the "Overall Metrics" tab.

Centralization   The extent to which some people are highly central (well connected) and others are not. Typically measured by the standard deviation of individual centralities (degree, betweenness, closeness).

In NodeXL: Frequency distributions of degree, betweenness, closeness, and eigenvector centrality are reported on the "Overall Metrics" tab after calculating Graph Metrics.

Isolate   A person in a network who is not connected to at least one other person.

Outlier   A person connected to only one other person; a peripheral member of a network.

In NodeXL: Isolates and outliers are evident when you draw a network graph.

Critical person   A person in a network who, when removed, causes one or more people to become isolated, or breaks the network into two or more disconnected regions.

*In NodeXL: Calculate centrality (as above) using Graph Metrics for the whole network. Then delete the node that interests you (the possible "critical person"; e.g., the one with the highest betweenness score) and Refresh Graph to see if (1) the network splits into separate components and/or (2) the average path length goes up dramatically without that person. **[Note: Save this as a new file after deleting a node.]***

Notes

Chapter 1

1. Debra E. Meyerson and Maureen A. Scully, "Tempered Radicalism and the Politics of Ambivalence and Change," *Organization Science* 6 (1995): 585–600.

2. The classic statement is Clayton M. Christensen, *The Innovator's Dilemma: When New Technologies Cause Great Firms to Fail* (1997; Boston: Harvard Business Review Press, 2013).

3. Ezra Pound, "Henry James" in *Literary Essays of Ezra Pound,* ed. T.S. Eliot (New York: New Directions, 1968).

4. Unless otherwise noted, quotations from social innovators are from personal interviews conducted by the authors between 2010 and 2014.

5. See Hayagreeva Rao, Calvin Morrill, and Mayer N. Zald "Power Plays: How Social Movements and Collective Action Create New Organizational Forms," *Research in Organizational Behavior* 22 (2000): 237–81.

6. See W. E. Douglas Creed, Maureen A. Scully, and John R. Austin, "Clothes Make the Person? The Tailoring of Legitimating Accounts and the Social Construction of Identity." *Organization Science* 13 (2002): 475–96.

7. Zald's now-classic work on this topic is Mayer N. Zald and Michael A. Berger, "Social Movements in organizations: Coup d'Etat, Insurgency, and Mass Movements," *American Journal of Sociology* 83 (1978): 823–61.

8. Peter Applebome and Elizabeth Maker, "At Newtown Starbucks, a Gun Event Is Shut Out," *New York Times,* August 10, 2013, www.nytimes.com/2013/08/10/nyregion/gun-rights-celebration-at-starbucks-not-in-newtown.html.

9. Howard Schultz, "An Open Letter from Howard Schultz, CEO of Starbucks Coffee Company," Starbucks blog, September 17, 2013, http://www.starbucks.com/blog/an-open-letter-from-howard-schultz/1268.

10. Andrew Garber, "Starbucks Supports Gay Marriage Legislation," *Seattle Times,* January 24, 2012, http://seattletimes.com/html/politics northwest/2017323520_starbucks_supports_gay_marriag.html.

11. See Alistair Barr, "Mozilla CEO Brendan Eich Steps Down," *Wall Street Journal,* April 3, 2014, http://online.wsj.com/news/articles/ SB10001424052702303532704579479741125367618.

12. For more on the "responsibility paradox," see Gerald F. Davis, Marina V. N. Whitman, and Mayer N. Zald, "The Responsibility Paradox." *Stanford Social Innovation Review* 6, no. 1 (2008): 30–37.

13. See Claire O'Connor, "Walmart Extends Benefits to LGBT Employees' Same-Sex Domestic Partners," *Forbes,* August 28, 2013, http://www.forbes.com/sites/clareoconnor/2013/08/28/walmart -extends-benefits-to-lgbt-employees-same-sex-domestic-partners/.

Chapter 2

1. Gifford Pinchot III and Elizabeth S. Pinchot, "Intracorporate Entrepreneurship," 1978, http://www.intrapreneur.com/MainPages /History/IntraCorp.html.

2. Fred Keller was influenced by the research of Ruby K. Payne. She and her coauthors describe the "Hidden Rules of Poverty" in Ruby K. Payne, Philip DeVol, and Terie Dreussi Smith, *Bridges Out of Poverty: Strategies for Professionals and Communities* (Houston, TX: Aha Process Inc., 2000).

3. Kevin Thompson's experience is described in Christopher Marquis and Rosabeth Moss Kanter, "IBM: The Corporate Service Corps," Harvard Business School case 409-106 (Boston: Harvard Business School Publishing, 2009).

Chapter 3

1. Pam Belluck, Jennifer Preston, and Gardiner Harris, "Cancer Group Backs Down on Cutting Off Planned Parenthood," *New York Times,* February 3, 2012, http://www.nytimes.com/2012/02/04 /health/policy/komen-breast-cancer-group-reverses-decision-that-cut -off-planned-parenthood.html?pagewanted=all&_r=0.

2. *Wikipedia,* s.v. "Social movement," last modified October 11, 2014, http://en.wikipedia.org/wiki/Social_movement.

3. The literature on social movements is vast. Classics include William Gamson, *The Strategy of Social Protest* (Homewood, IL: Dorsey, 1975); John D. McCarthy and Mayer N. Zald, "Resource Mobilization Theory and Social Movements: A Partial Theory," *American Journal of Sociology* 82 (1977): 1212–41; Charles Tilly, *From Mobilization to Revolution* (Reading, MA: Addison-Wesley, 1978); Doug McAdam, *Political Process and the Development of Black Insurgency, 1930–1970,* rev. ed. (Chicago: University of Chicago Press, 1999); David A. Snow and Robert D. Benford, "Ideology, Frame Resonance, and Participant Mobilization." *International Social Movement Research* 1 (1988): 197–217. For overviews, see Sidney Tarrow, *Power in Movement* (New York: Cambridge University Press, 1994); and Doug McAdam, John D. McCarthy, and Mayer N. Zald, eds., *Comparative Perspectives on Social Movements: Political Opportunities, Mobilizing Structures, and Cultural Framings* (New York: Cambridge University Press, 1996).

4. Clay Shirky, *Here Comes Everybody: The Power of Organizing Without Organizations* (New York: Penguin, 2008).

5. Mayer N. Zald and Michael A. Berger, "Social Movements in Organizations: Coup d'Etat, Insurgency, and Mass Movements," *American Journal of Sociology* 83 (1978): 823–61.

6. Landon Thomas Jr., "John Mack Is Back at Morgan Stanley," *New York Times,* July 1, 2005, http://www.nytimes.com/2005/06/30 /business/worldbusiness/30iht-morgan.html.

7. Michael Moss "HealthSouth's CEO Exposes, Sues Anonymous Online Critics," *Wall Street Journal,* July 7, 1999, http://online.wsj .com/news/articles/SB93130273468312859; and Carrick Mollenkamp, "An Accountant Tried in Vain to Expose HealthSouth Fraud," *Wall Street Journal,* May 20, 2003, http://online.wsj.com/news/articles /SB105338447947754000.

8. "Wal-Mart Offers Same-Sex Benefits as Corporate Bellwether," *benefitnews,* August 28, 2003, http://www.benefitnews.com/news /walmart-offers-same-sex-benefits-corporate-bellwether-2735714-1 .html.

9. Samuel J. Palmisano, "The Globally Integrated Enterprise." *Foreign Affairs* 85, no. 3 (May/June 2006), http://www.foreignaffairs

.com/articles/61713/samuel-j-palmisano/the-globally-integrated
-enterprise.

10. Anton Troianovski and Sven Grundberg, "Nokia's Bad Call on Smartphones," *Wall Street Journal,* July 18, 2012, http://online.wsj.com /news/articles/SB10001424052702304388004577531002591315494.

11. Malcolm Gladwell, *The Tipping Point: How Little Things Can Make a Big Difference* (Boston: Back Bay Books, 2001).

12. See Aldon D. Morris, *Origins of the Civil Rights Movement* (New York: Simon & Schuster, 1986).

13. David Wolman, "The Digital Road to Egypt's Revolution," *New York Times,* February 12, 2012, Sunday Review section, http:// www.nytimes.com/interactive/2012/02/12/opinion/sunday/20120212 -tahir-timeline.html.

Chapter 4

1. Joe Sharkey, "Reinventing the Suitcase by Adding the Wheel," *New York Times,* October 4, 2010, http://www.nytimes. com/2010/10/05/business/05road.html.

2. Doug McAdam, *Political Process and the Development of Black Insurgency, 1930–1970,* rev. ed. (Chicago: University of Chicago Press, 1999).

3. "The Shoe-Thrower's Index: An index of unrest in the Arab world," *The Economist online,* February 9, 2011, http://www.economist .com/blogs/dailychart/2011/02/daily_chart_arab_unrest_index.

4. Clare O'Connor, "Walmart Extends Benefits To LGBT Employees' Same-Sex Domestic Partners," *Forbes,* August 28, 2013, http://www.forbes.com/sites/clareoconnor/2013/08/28/walmart -extends-benefits-to-lgbt-employees-same-sex-domestic-partners/.

5. Kat Kinsman, "Activists Call Foul on KFC Bucket Campaign," *CNN.com,* April 28, 2010, http://www.cnn.com/2010/LIVING/ homestyle/04/28/kfc.pink.bucket.campaign/.

6. For a quick overview and tutorial on using ED, see http://www .sec.gov/investor/pubs/edgarguide.htm.

7. Apple Inc. SEC form 10-K, for fiscal year ending September 12, 2012. Accessed October 15, 2014. http://www.sec.gov/Archives /edgar/data/320193/000119312512444068/d411355d10k.htm.

8. Ibid.

9. Pfizer Inc. SEC Schedule 14A (Proxy Statement for 2013 Annual Shareholders Meeting), accessed October 15, 2014, http:// www.sec.gov/Archives/edgar/data/78003/000093041313001646 /c72654_def14a.htm.

10. Ibid.

11. Peter F. Drucker, "Drucker on Management: A Turnaround Primer," *Wall Street Journal,* February 2, 1993, http://online.wsj.com /news/articles/SB10001424052748704204304574544302267861062.

12. Edgar H. Schein, *Organizational Culture and Leadership* (San Francisco: Jossey-Bass, 1984).

13. For single words, try http://www.writewords.org.uk/word _count.asp; for phrases, try http://www.writewords.org.uk/phrase _count.asp. Also see http://www.semantic-knowledge.com/index .htm to download the free "Tropes" software for text analysis.

14. Klaus Weber, "Converging Orders of Worth: Adaptive and Demographic Mechanisms of Cultural Globalization," Kellogg School of Management Working Paper, 2013.

15. http://www.google.com/about/company/philosophy/.

16. Adam Bryant, "Sure, Take Me On. You Might Get a Promotion," *New York Times,* January 8, 2011, http://www.nytimes .com/2011/01/09/business/09corner.html.

17. Adam Bryant, "Bernard Tyson of Kaiser Permanente, on Speaking Your Mind," *New York Times,* November 9, 2013, http:// www.nytimes.com/2013/11/10/business/bernard-tyson-of-kaiser -permanente-on-speaking-your-mind.html.

18. See Christopher Marquis, "Driving Sustainability at Bloomberg LP," Harvard Business School case 9-411-025 (Boston: Harvard Business School, 2010).

19. Peter Elkind and Jennifer Reingold, "Inside Pfizer's Palace Coup," *Fortune,* July 28, 2011, http://features.blogs.fortune.cnn .com/2011/07/28/pfizer-jeff-kindler-shakeup/.

20. For a description of Truman's brief membership in the Klan (Truman quickly backed out when he realized the group was anti-Catholic), see Peter M. Carozzo, "Harry Truman and Civil Rights," *H-Net.org,* June 2002, http://www.h-net.org/reviews/showrev .php?id=6354. On Truman's attitudes toward minorities, see Peter J. Kuznick, "We Can Learn a Lot from Truman the Bigot," *Los Angeles*

Times, July 18, 2003, http://articles.latimes.com/2003/jul/18/opinion
/oe-kuznick18.

21. Julie Froud, Johal Sukhdev, Adam Leaver, and Karel Williams,
Financialization and Strategy: Narrative and Numbers (London:
Routledge, 2006).

22. Doug McAdam, John D. McCarthy, and Mayer N. Zald, eds.,
*Comparative Perspectives on Social Movements: Political Opportunities,
Mobilizing Structures, and Cultural Framings* (New York: Cambridge
University Press, 1996).

23. John Maynard Keynes, *The General Theory of Employment,
Interest, and Money* (London: Palgrave MacMillan, 1936).

24. An excellent website for tracking who is doing what in this
domain is www.business-humanrights.org. An innovator hoping to
advocate for her company to adopt a human rights code will find over
three hundred examples of other companies' codes here, providing an
array of supporting material for their initiatives.

25. Forrest Briscoe and Sean Safford, "The Nixon-in-China Effect:
Activism, Imitation, and the Institutionalization of Contentious
Practices," *Administrative Science Quarterly* 53 (2008): 460–91.

26. Isaiah Berlin, *The Hedgehog and the Fox* (New York: Simon &
Schuster, 1953). Excerpted at http://www.design.caltech.edu/erik
/Misc/Fox_Hedgehog.html.

Chapter 5

1. Jim Avila, "70 Percent of Ground Beef at Supermarkets Contains
'Pink Slime,'" *ABC News.com,* March 7, 2012, http://abcnews.go.com
/blogs/headlines/2012/03/70-percent-of-ground-beef-at-supermarkets
-contains-pink-slime/.

2. "'It's 100 Percent Beef': Company on Defensive as It Closes
Plants," *ABC News.com,* January 9, 2010.

3. P. J. Huffstutter and Lisa Baertlein, "'Pink Slime' Controversy
Stokes Clash over Agriculture," *Reuters.com,* April 4, 2012, http://
www.reuters.com/article/2012/04/16/us-usa-agriculture-clash
-idUSBRE83F05E20120416.

4. Communications, "2012 Election Spending Will Reach
$6 Billion, Center for Responsive Politics Predicts," *OpenSecrets,*

October 31, 2012, http://www.opensecrets.org/news/2012/10/2012
-election-spending-will-reach-6.html.

5. Susan J. Ashford, "Championing Charged Issues: The Case
of Gender Equity within Organizations," *Power and Influence in Organizations,* ed. R.M. Kramer and M. A. Neale (Thousand Oaks, CA:
Sage, 1998), 349–80.

6. https://twitter.com/gselevator.

7. Christopher Marquis, "Goldman Sachs: The 10,000 Women
Initiative," Harvard Business School case 5-09-042 (Boston: Harvard
Business School, July 2010).

8. Jon Ronson, "Watch: The Story of a Man Who Faked Insanity,"
Huffington Post, March 28, 2013, http://www.huffingtonpost.com
/jon-ronson/psychopath-test-ted-talk_b_2973423.html.

9. Jane E. Dutton, Susan J. Ashford, Regina M. O'Neill, and
Katherine A. Lawrence, "Moves That Matter: Issue Selling and
Organizational Change," *Academy of Management Journal* 44 (2001):
716–736.

10. Debra Meyerson, *Tempered Radicals: How Everyday Leaders Inspire
Change at Work* (Boston: Harvard Business School Publishing, 2003).

11. The skills of a social intrapreneur are comparable to those of a
social entrepreneur. Robert Chatwani also started a social movement
in support of an issue that was highly personal for him. His request for
help to find a bone marrow match for his friend Samir Bhatia received
an enormous response. Indeed, the story of Chatwani's efforts became
the central example used in Jennifer Aaker and Andy Smith, *The
Dragonfly Effect: Quick, Effective, and Powerful Ways to Use Social Media
to Drive Social Change* (San Francisco: Jossey-Bass, 2010).

12. "Clever Little Bag," *Fuse Project*, accessed October 17, 2014,
http://www.fuseproject.com/products-47.

13. Katherine Burson, Robert Smith, and David Faro, "The Influence of Victim-Unitization on Charitable Giving," *European Advances
in Consumer Research,* vol. 9, ed. Alan Bradshaw, Chris Hackley, and
Pauline Maclaran (Duluth, MN: Association for Consumer Research,
2011), 515.

14. Jyllian Kemsley, "Dow Chemical Teams Up With Universities
On Laboratory Safety," *Chemical and Engineering News,* October 29,
2012, http://cen.acs.org/articles/90/i44/Dow-Chemical-Teams
-Universities-Laboratory.html.

15. "Safety Matters: Dow Goes On a Lab Safety Mission to Benefit the Future Chemical Workforce," Dow website, accessed October 17, 2014, http://www.dow.com/innovation/featured_articles/labsafety.htm.

16. Ernesto Londano, "Egyptian Man's Death Became Symbol of Callous State," *Washington Post,* February 9, 2011, http://www.washingtonpost.com/wp-dyn/content/article/2011/02/08/AR2011020806360.html.

17. Will Heaven, "Egypt and Facebook: time to update its status?" NATO Review website, accessed October 17, 2014, http://www.nato.int/docu/review/2011/Social_Medias/Egypt_Facebook/EN/index.htm.

Chapter 6

1. This story is drawn from Bill Breen and Cheryl Dahle, "Fire Starters," *Fast Company,* November 9, 1999, http://www.fastcompany.com/38400/fire-starters.

2. For an excellent overview, see Martin Kilduff and Wenpin Tsai, *Social Networks and Organizations* (London: Sage, 2003).

3. Siobhan Gorman, Adam Entous, and Andrew Dowell, "Technology Emboldened the NSA," *Wall Street Journal,* June 9, 2013, http://online.wsj.com/news/articles/SB10001424127887323495604578535290627442964?mg=reno64-wsj#printMode.

4. Duncan Watts, *"Small Worlds: The Dynamics of Networks between Order and Randomness* (Princeton, NJ: Princeton University Press, 2003).

5. Gerald F. Davis, Mina Yoo, and Wayne E. Baker, "The Small World of the American Corporate Elite, 1982–2001," *Strategic Organization* 1 (2003): 301–26.

6. Doug McAdam, "Recruitment to High-Risk Activism: The Case of Freedom Summer," *American Journal of Sociology* 92 (1986): 64–90.

7. Ronald S. Burt, *Structural Holes* (Cambridge, MA: Harvard University Press, 1992).

8. *Wikipedia,* s.v. "Enron Corpus," last modified June 17, 2014, http://en.wikipedia.org/wiki/Enron_Corpus.

9. The authoritative source here is Stanley Wasserman and Katherine Faust, *Social Network Analysis: Methods and Applications* (New York: Cambridge University Press, 1994).

10. Jean Wineman, Felichism Kabo, and Gerald F. Davis, "Spatial and Social Networks in Organizational Innovation," *Environment and Behavior* 41, no. 3 (2009): 427–42.

11. Forrest Briscoe and Wenpin Tsai, "Overcoming Relational Inertia: How Organizational Members Respond to Acquisition Events in a Law Firm," *Administrative Science Quarterly* 56 (2011): 408–40.

12. Malcolm Gladwell, *The Tipping Point: How Little Things Can Make a Big Difference* (Boston: Back Bay Books, 2001).

13. McAdam, "Recruitment to High-Risk Activism."

14. Maureen A. Scully and W. E. Douglas Creed "Subverting Our stories of Subversion," in Gerald F. Davis, Doug McAdam, W. Richard Scott, and Mayer N. Zald, eds., *Social Movements and Organization Theory* (New York: Cambridge University Press, 2005).

15. Kieran Healy, "Using Metadata to Find Paul Revere," *Slate*, June 10, 2013, http://www.slate.com/articles/health_and_science /science/2013/06/prism_metadata_analysis_paul_revere_identified _by_his_connections_to_other.html.

Chapter 7

1. Peter Goodspeed, "The Arab Awakening: The Ex-Google Executive behind Egypt's Online Revolution," *National Post*, December 19, 2011, http://fullcomment.nationalpost.com/2011 /12/19/61518/.

2. Clay Shirky, *Here Comes Everybody: The Power of Organizing Without Organizations* (New York: Penguin, 2008).

3. "The Technology Helping Repressive Regimes Spy," Ben Elgin, interview by Dave Davies, *Fresh Air*, December 13, 2011, http://www .npr.org/2011/12/14/143639670/the-technology-helping-repressive -regimes-spy.

4. Ben Elgin, Vernon Silver and Alan Katz, "Iranian Police Seizing Dissidents Get Aid of Western Companies," *Bloomberg*, October 30, 2011, http://www.bloomberg.com/news/2011-10-31/iranian-police -seizing-dissidents-get-aid-of-western-companies.html.

5. "CIA's 'Facebook' Program Dramatically Cut Agency's Costs," *The Onion*, http://www.theonion.com/video/cias-facebook-program -dramatically-cut-agencys-cos,19753/.

Notes

6. Robert D. Putnam, *Bowling Alone: The Collapse and Revival of American Community* (New York: Simon and Schuster, 2000).

7. Christopher Marquis, Gerald F. Davis, and MaryAnn Glynn, "Golfing Alone? Corporations, Elites, and Nonprofit Growth in 100 American Communities," *Organization Science* 24, no. 1 (2013): 39–57; Mary Ann Glynn, "Configuring the Field of Play: How Hosting the Olympic Games Impacts Civic Community," *Journal of Management Studies* 45 (2008): 1117–1146.

8. Aldon Morris, "Black Southern Student Sit-In Movement: An Analysis of Internal Organization" *American Sociological Review* 46 (1981): 744–67.

9. Ibid.

10. See Sidney Tarrow, *Power in Movement* (New York: Cambridge University Press, 1994).

11. For an authoritative account, see Jennifer Earl and Katrina Kimport, *Digitally Enabled Social Change: Activism in the Internet Age* (Cambridge, MA: MIT Press, 2011).

12. Ibid.

13. Victoria McGrane, "Chamber Launches 'Virtual March' on Finance Bill," *Wall Street Journal*, June 21, 2010, http://online.wsj.com /news/articles/SB10001424052748704895204575321251086879046.

14. Ned Potter, "SOPA Blackout: Wikipedia, Google, Wired protest 'Internet Censorship,'" *ABC News.com*, January 18, 2012, http://abcnews.go.com/blogs/technology/2012/01/sopa-blackout -wikipedia-google-wired-join-protest-against-internet-censorship/.

15. Janine Di Giovanni, "The Quiet American," *New York Times T Magazine*, September 3, 2012, http://www.nytimes .com/2012/09/09/t-magazine/gene-sharp-theorist-of-power .html?pagewanted=all&_r=0.

16. Goodspeed, "The Arab Awakening."

17. Evgeny Morozov, *The Net Delusion: The Dark Side of Internet Freedom* (New York: Public Affairs, 2011).

18. "Commotion Wireless," on Open Technology Institute website, accessed October 17, 2014, http://oti.newamerica.net/ commotion_wireless_0.

19. "Electronic Ties That Bind," *The Economist*, June 25, 2009, http://www.economist.com/node/13915798.

20. Joel Schechtman, "IBM Security Tool Can Flag 'Disgruntled Employees,'" *CIO Journal* (blog), *Wall Street Journal*, January 29, 2013, http://blogs.wsj.com/cio/2013/01/29/ibm-security-tool-can-flag -disgruntled-employees/.

21. Michael Moss "HealthSouth's CEO Exposes, Sues Anonymous Online Critics," *Wall Street Journal*, July 7, 1999, http://online.wsj. com/news/articles/SB93130273468312859; Carrick Mollenkamp, "An Accountant Tried in Vain to Expose HealthSouth Fraud," *Wall Street Journal*, May 20, 2003, http://online.wsj.com/news/articles /SB105338447947754000.

Chapter 8

1. David Streitfeld, "Airbnb Takes to the Barricades," *New York Times*, April 29, 2014, http://bits.blogs.nytimes.com/2014/04/29 /airbnb-takes-to-the-barricades/.

2. Schanberg, Sydney H., "On the playgrounds of America, every kid's goal is to score: in Pakistan, where children stitch soccer balls for six cents an hour, the goal is to survive." *Life Magazine* (June 1996), 38–48.

3. Shelley Banjo, "Inside Nike's Struggle to Balance Cost and Worker Safety in Bangladesh," *Wall Street Journal*, April 21, 2014, http://online.wsj.com/news/articles/SB100014240527023038736045 79493502231397942.

4. The case of Ramón de Mendiola and Florida Ice & Farm is well described in Subramanian Rangan's two INSEAD cases, "Florida Ice & Farm Co A: 2003–2008" and "Florida Ice & Farm Co B: 2009–2013."

5. Gerald F. Davis, "Agents without Principles? The Spread of the Poison Pill through the Intercorporate Network," *Administrative Science Quarterly* 36, no. 4 (December 1991): 583–613.

6. Kofi Annan, remarks to United States Chamber of Commerce, Washington, D.C., June 5, 2001, http://www.unis.unvienna.org/unis /en/pressrels/2001/sgsm7827.html.

Bibliography

Aaker, Jennifer, and Andy Smith. *The Dragonfly Effect: Quick, Effective, and Powerful Ways to Use Social Media to Drive Social Change.* San Francisco: Jossey-Bass, 2010.

Arena, Christine. *The High-Purpose Company: The Truly Responsible (and Highly Profitable) Firms That Are Changing Business Now.* New York: HarperBusiness, 2006.

Ashford, Susan J., and James Detert. "Selling Ideas Up the Chain of Command: Tactics for leading change from the middle of your organization." *Harvard Business Review,* forthcoming.

Benford, Robert B., and David A. Snow. "Framing Processes and Social Movements: An Overview and Assessment." *Annual Review of Sociology* 26 (2000): 611–39.

Benkler, Yochai. *The Penguin and the Leviathan: How Cooperation Triumphs over Self-Interest.* New York: Crown Business, 2011.

Bornstein, David, and Susan Davis. *Social Entrepreneurship: What Everyone Needs to Know.* New York: Oxford University Press, 2010.

Briscoe, Forrest, and Sean Safford. "The Nixon-in-China Effect: Activism, Imitation, and the Institutionalization of Contentious Practices." *Administrative Science Quarterly* 53 (2008): 460–91.

Clemens, Elisabeth S. *The People's Lobby: Organizational Innovation and the Rise of Interest Group Politics in the United States, 1890–1925.* Chicago: University of Chicago Press, 1997.

Creed, W. E. Douglas, Maureen A. Scully, and John R. Austin. "Clothes Make the Person? The Tailoring of Legitimating Accounts and the Social Construction of Identity." *Organization Science* 13 (2002): 475–96.

Davis, Gerald F. *Managed by the Markets: How Finance Reshaped America.* New York: Oxford University Press, 2009.

Davis, Gerald F., Doug McAdam, W. Richard Scott, and Mayer N. Zald, eds. *Social Movements and Organization Theory.* New York: Cambridge University Press, 2005.

Bibliography

Dutton, Jane E., Susan J. Ashford, Regina M. O'Neill, and Katherine A. Lawrence. "Moves That Matter: Issue Selling and Organizational Change." *Academy of Management Journal* 44 (2001): 716–36.

Earl, Jennifer, and Katrina Kimport. *Digitally Enabled Social Change: Activism in the Internet Age*. Cambridge, MA: MIT Press, 2011.

Elkington, John and Pamela Hartigan. *The Power of Unreasonable People: How Social Entrepreneurs Create Markets That Change the World*. Boston: Harvard Business Press, 2008.

Gamson, William. *The Strategy of Social Protest*. Homewood, IL: Dorsey, 1975.

Giugni, Marco. "Was It Worth the Effort? The Outcomes and Consequences of Social Movements." *Annual Review of Sociology* 98 (1998): 371–93.

Giugni, Marco, Doug McAdam, and Charles Tilly. *How Movements Matter*. Minneapolis: University of Minnesota Press, 1999.

Gladwell, Malcolm. *The Tipping Point: How Little Things Make a Big Difference*. Boston: Back Bay Books, 2002.

Godin, Seth. *Linchpin: Are You Indispensable?* New York: Random House, 2008.

Grenny, Joseph, Kerry Patterson, David Maxfield, Ron McMillan, and Al Switzer. *Influencer: The New Science of Leading Change*. New York: McGraw-Hill, 2013.

Hansen, Derek, Ben Shneiderman, and Marc A. Smith. *Analyzing Social Media Networks with NodeXL: Insights from a Connected World*. Burlington, MA: Morgan Kaufmann, 2010.

Hart, Stuart. *Capitalism at the Crossroads*. Philadelphia: Wharton Publishing, 2005.

Haydu, Jeffrey. "Counter Action Frames: Employer Repertoires and the Union Menace in the Late Nineteenth Century." *Social Problems* 46 (1999): 313–31.

Heath, Chip and Dan Heath. *Made to Stick: Why Some Ideas Survive and Others Die*. New York: Random House, 2007.

Hoffman, Andrew J. *From Heresy to Dogma: An Institutional History of Corporate Environmentalism*. San Francisco: New Lexington Press, 1997.

Kahneman, Daniel. *Thinking, Fast and Slow*. New York: Farrar, Straus, and Giroux, 2013.

Klandermans, Bert. *The Social Psychology of Protest*. Oxford, UK, and Cambridge, MA: Blackwell, 1997.

McAdam, Doug. *Political Process and the Development of Black Insurgency, 1930–1970*. Chicago: University of Chicago Press, 1982.

———."Recruitment to High-Risk Activism: The Case of Freedom Summer." *American Journal of Sociology* 92 (1986): 64–90.

McAdam, Doug , John D. McCarthy, and Mayer N. Zald, eds. *Comparative Perspectives on Social Movements: Political Opportunities, Mobilizing Structures, and Cultural Framings*. New York: Cambridge University Press, 1996.

McCann, Michael W. *Rights at Work: Pay Equity Reform and the Politics of Legal Mobilization*. Chicago: University of Chicago Press, 1994.

McCarthy, John D., and Mayer N. Zald. "Resource Mobilization Theory and Social Movements: A Partial Theory." *American Journal of Sociology* 82 (1977): 1212–41.

Meyerson, Debra E. *Tempered Radicals: How People use Difference to Inspire Change at Work*. Boston: Harvard Business School Publishing, 2001.

Meyerson, Debra E., and Maureen A. Scully. "Tempered Radicalism and the Politics of Ambivalence and Change." *Organization Science* 6 (1995): 585–600.

Morris, Aldon. "Black Southern Student Sit-In Movement: An Analysis of Internal Organization." *American Sociological Review* 46 (1981): 744–67.

———. *The Origins of the Civil Rights Movement: Black Communities Organizing for Change*. New York: Free Press, 1984.

Thaler, Richard H., and Cass R. Sunstein. *Nudge: Improving Decisions About Health, Wealth, and Happiness*. New York: Penguin Books, 2009.

Raeburn, Nicole C. *Changing Corporate America from Inside Out*. Minneapolis: University of Minnesota Press, 2004.

Rao, Hayagreeva. *Market Rebels: How Activists Make or Break Radical Innovations*. Princeton: Princeton University Press, 2008.

Rao, Hayagreeva, Calvin Morrill, and Mayer N. Zald. "Power Plays: Social Movements, Collective Action and New Organizational Forms." *Research in Organizational Behavior* 22 (2000): 237–82.

Shirky, Clay. *Here Comes Everybody: The Power of Organization Without Organizations*. New York: Penguin, 2009.

Bibliography

Snow, David A., and Sarah A. Soule. *A Primer on Social Movements*. New York: W. W. Norton, 2009.

Soule, Sarah A. *Contention and Corporate Social Responsibility*. New York: Cambridge University Press, 2009.

Spreitzer, Gretchen, and Christine Porath. "Creating Sustainable Performance." *Harvard Business Review*, January–February 2012, 92–99.

Tarrow, Sidney. *Power in Movement*. New York: Cambridge University Press, 1994.

Tilly, Charles. *From Mobilization to Revolution*. Reading, MA: Addison-Wesley, 1978.

Zald, Mayer N., and Michael Berger. "Social Movements in Organizations: Coup d'Etat, Bureaucratic Insurgency, and Mass Rebellions." *American Journal of Sociology* 83 (1978): 823–61.

Zald, Mayer N., and John D. McCarthy. *Social Movements in an Organizational Society*. New Brunswick, NJ: Transaction, 1987.

Index

Vietnam, 91
virtual protests, 132–133

Walmart, 13, 35, 49
Weber, Klaus, 63, 85
Weill, Sandy, 68
Welfare-to-Career program
    (Cascade Engineering),
    20–23, 98–99
Whitman, Meg, 89
Whole Foods Market, 5–6, 19,
    28, 62, 87, 149
Wikipedia, 134
World of Good (eBay), 17–18,
    89–90

Xerox, 4

Yahoo Finance, 140, 141
Yammer, 142
YES Florida (Florida Ice &
    Farm Company),
    150–151
YouTube, 44, 136

Zald, Mayer, 9, 34

Acknowledgments

We were fortunate to have the opportunity to speak with dozens of social intrapreneurs in teaching our class and writing this book. Many of them are named in the text; others remain anonymous. Among many others, we would like to recognize David Berdish, Gib Bulloch, Robert Chatwani, Justin DeKoszmovszky, Fred Keller, Joe Malcoun, Marcos Mancini, Walter Robb, and Kevin Thompson. We are grateful to all of them for their help and insights.

We would also like to thank our recovering students, who have helped us to refine our thinking and approach through their engagement in the classroom and in the hallways. We are proud that they are now putting these frameworks and tools into practice in their organizations. In particular, we give recognition to our teaching assistants Sabrina Sullivan and Sheena Van Leuven.

We also thank a number of people who read and commented on the text, including Katharine Bierce, Doug Creed, and Klaus Weber. Of course, they should be held blameless for anything that doesn't work.

Finally, we are grateful to the Ross School of Business for providing support in countless ways to make this book possible and providing a nurturing environment for positive business in theory and in practice.

About the Authors

Gerald F. Davis is the Wilbur K. Pierpont Collegiate Professor of Management at the University of Michigan's Ross School of Business and professor of sociology at the University of Michigan. He is editor of the *Administrative Science Quarterly* and director of the Interdisciplinary Committee on Organization Studies (ICOS) at Michigan. His most recent book was *Managed by the Markets: How Finance Re-Shaped America*, which won the Academy of Management's Terry Award for Outstanding Contribution to Management Knowledge in 2010.

Christopher J. White is Managing Director of the Center for Positive Organizations and adjunct faculty in Management & Organizations at the University of Michigan's Ross School of Business. The Center has been recognized by the Academy of Management with awards for opening a new field of inquiry within management science and for impact on management practices. He has been leading and consulting to purpose-driven organizations, spanning the corporate, nonprofit, and philanthropic sectors, for over fifteen years.